OUTER ORDER, INNER CALM

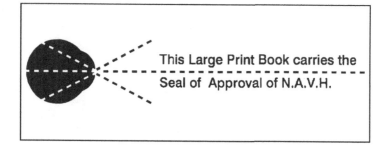

This Large Print Book carries the
Seal of Approval of N.A.V.H.

Outer Order, Inner Calm

DECLUTTER & ORGANIZE TO MAKE MORE ROOM FOR HAPPINESS

Gretchen Rubin

THORNDIKE PRESS
A part of Gale, a Cengage Company

Farmington Hills, Mich • San Francisco • New York • Waterville, Maine
Meriden, Conn • Mason, Ohio • Chicago

Copyright © 2019 by Gretchen Rubin.
Illustrations by Jon McNaught.
Thorndike Press, a part of Gale, a Cengage Company.

LIBRARY OF CONGRESS CIP DATA ON FILE.
CATALOGUING IN PUBLICATION FOR THIS BOOK
IS AVAILABLE FROM THE LIBRARY OF CONGRESS

ISBN-13: 978-1-4328-6373-9 (hardcover alk. paper)

Published in 2019 by arrangement with Harmony Books, an imprint of Random House, a division of Penguin Random House LLC

Printed in Mexico
1 2 3 4 5 6 7 23 22 21 20 19

To my readers, listeners, and viewers

Order is Heaven's first law.

ALEXANDER POPE

CONTENTS

■ ■ ■ ■

INTRODUCTION: WHY BOTHER WITH OUTER ORDER?

■ ■ ■ ■

In my study of happiness, I've realized that for most of us, *outer order contributes to inner calm.*

More than it should.

In the context of a happy life, a messy desk or a crowded coat closet is a trivial problem — yet getting control of the *stuff* of life often makes it easier to feel more in control of our lives generally.

When I'm surrounded by a mess, I feel restless and unsettled. When I clean up that mess, I'm always surprised by the disproportionate energy and cheer I gain, plus I'm able to find my keys. A friend once told me, "I finally cleaned out my fridge and now I know I can switch careers." I knew *exactly* what she meant.

By getting rid of the things I don't use, don't need, or don't love, as well as the things that don't work, don't fit, or don't suit, I free my mind — and my shelves — for what I truly value. And that's true for most people.

Often, when disorder starts to creep in, I think, I don't have time to fight my way through all this stuff! I'm too busy to deal with it! But I've learned that by managing my possessions, I can improve my emotional attitude, my physical health, my intellectual vigor, and even my social life.

Now, no matter how busy I am, I force myself to take at least a few minutes each day to impose some order. If I'm feeling overwhelmed by multiple writing deadlines, I spend twenty minutes cleaning my office, because I know that clearing my papers clears my mind.

I've also found that once I start, it's easier to keep going. True, sometimes it feels auspicious to do a big clutter-clearing on New Year's Day, or as spring cleaning, or as pre–Labor Day prep — but *now* is always the best time to begin. A friend told me, "I woke up one morning and on impulse decided to tackle my basement. I spent my entire Sunday down there, and I was so pumped by the end that I wanted to keep going all night. I got up early on Monday morning just to sit there and gloat. It gave me such a lift at the start of a tough work-week."

We want to cherish our possessions and we also want to feel free of them. I want to keep every toy that my children ever loved, but I also want to have plenty of space in our apartment.

With outer order, we achieve that balance.

Outer order offers nine promises:

1

OUTER ORDER SAVES TIME, MONEY, SPACE, ENERGY, AND PATIENCE. I move more smoothly through my days. I don't waste time searching for things; I don't struggle to put things away; I don't have to run out to buy a duplicate of something I already own. It's easier to clean. I feel less frustrated, less rushed, and less cramped. I'm not frittering my life away on trivial chores and annoyances.

2

OUTER ORDER FOSTERS PEACE WITHIN RELATIONSHIPS. I spend less time nagging at or arguing with other people. I avoid boring questions like "Where's my passport?" "Where's the toner?" "Who left the mess in that room?" "Where does this go?"

15

3

OUTER ORDER CREATES A FEELING OF SANCTUARY. I experience true leisure because I don't feel pressured to jump up and deal with a mess. Once visual noise is eliminated, I feel more focused and there's more room in my mind, my schedule, and my space for creative activity. Instead of being sources of stress, my home and my office are places of comfort and energy. I can revel in the beauty of my possessions because I can see and reach everything easily. I have plenty of room for everything that's important to me. Our physical experience colors our emotional experience, and when my body is in a place that's orderly, my mind becomes more serene.

4

OUTER ORDER REDUCES GUILT. I feel relieved of guilt about the possessions I've never used and the projects I've never finished. Because I make better use of what I already own, I can buy less in the future. And I know I'll leave a lighter burden for others to handle after I'm gone.

5

OUTER ORDER ALLOWS ME TO PRO-
JECT A MORE POSITIVE IDENTITY
TO MYSELF AND TO THE WORLD. I
feel greater self-possession; I feel more self-
assured and capable. Once I've cleared away
the things I don't need, use, or love, my surroundings reveal to me, and to others, the
things that matter most to me. Careful curation means that my space and my possessions reflect my truest identity.

6

OUTER ORDER RELIEVES ME OF
THE FEAR OF PEOPLE'S JUDGMENT.
I'm more hospitable because I can invite
people over without hours of preparatory
cleaning. I don't panic at the prospect of an
unexpected guest or an emergency repair.
I'm pleased to show my space to others.

7

OUTER ORDER REFLECTS WHAT'S
HAPPENING NOW IN MY LIFE. Be-
cause I've let go of things that once — but
no longer — played an active role in my life,
I have more time for what's important right
now. No more giant toys from my children's
babyhood, no more rows of thick law books
crowding my office bookshelves. I keep a

few precious mementos from the old days, but most of my space is devoted to what's important *now.*

8

OUTER ORDER CREATES A SENSE OF POSSIBILITY. When too much stuff piles up, I feel paralyzed. Digging myself out of the mess seems insurmountable, so I stay stuck. When clutter is gone, I have more choices about the future: what to buy, what to do, where and how to live. Because I'm no longer hemmed in by possessions, I feel a sense of renewal.

9

OUTER ORDER SHARPENS MY SENSE OF PURPOSEFULNESS. I know what I have, why I have it, and where it belongs. I make good use of everything I own. There's nothing random, no uncertainty, no default choices. I'm surrounded by meaningful possessions that are ready for me to use them.

Our rooms shape our thoughts, and our possessions change our moods. It can be challenging to influence our thoughts and actions directly; by improving the state of our surroundings, we can improve our state of mind.

Because our minds feed on the experience of our five senses, pleasing our senses raises our spirits.

Given how much clutter affects my own happiness and the enthusiasm for this subject in popular culture, I'm surprised that researchers haven't investigated the effects of clutter more thoroughly. The studies that do exist tend to address questions such as whether it's "better" to be organized or messy. To me, the answer seems obvious: *It depends.* We all differ in what works "better."

We all must face clutter in the way *that's right for us.* We're all different — in what possessions we value, in the kinds of surroundings that we find pleasurable, in the kinds of habits that come naturally to us, in the dynamics of our household or workplace. There's no one "right" or "best" way to create a better life.

In fact, we should work to create outer order only if it makes us happier. There's no magic in making a bed, or filing papers, or emptying an in-box each night. These efforts are worthwhile only if they bring us more happiness. We've achieved the right level of order when we can find what we need, feel good in our space, and don't feel hindered by stuff. For some people, what

19

looks like disorder works just fine.

Why, then, do so many experts insist that they've found the one true and right way? It's a fact about human nature: when *getting* advice, we love to receive a precise, standardized template for success, and when *giving* advice, we love to insist that the strategy that works so well for us will surely work for others. *But each of us must find our own way.*

Some people want to clear a little clutter each day; some people want to work for fourteen hours straight. Some people struggle with overbuying; some people (like me) struggle with underbuying. Some people feel a strong emotional or mystical attachment to possessions; others don't feel much connection to objects. Some people curate their possessions with great care; others put little thought into what they buy and where they put it. Some people are powerfully attracted by the promise of minimalism — and some people aren't.

Nevertheless, while each of us might define and achieve outer order in different ways, it's clear that for most people, outer order does indeed contribute to inner calm.

Some people ask me, "Given the problems of the world, isn't it superficial and silly to devote time, energy, money, or concern to tackling clutter?" We may be deeply worried about the problems of the world, and we're *right* to be worried. Yet the promise of outer order is something that we can tackle on our own right now. By doing so, we help restore our equanimity — and this isn't a futile or selfish gesture, because that equanimity makes us more effective when we seek to address the problems of the world.

Outer Order, Inner Calm lays out the five stages for establishing outer order. First, we *make choices* — what possessions to keep and what to do with them. Once we've cleared through our things, we *create order* by organizing, repairing, and attending to neglected areas. Next, we reflect on ourselves, to *know ourselves — and others* — so that we can take those individual insights into account. Then, once the clutter is vanquished, it's useful to *cultivate helpful habits* to maintain that order, so the clutter doesn't return. The fifth and final step is to *add beauty* to make our surroundings more inviting and comfortable.

The chapters covering these five stages encompass a wide range of suggestions about how to create outer order. Different ideas appeal to different people, and each reader can adopt those ideas that strike a chord — and ignore the ones that don't resonate. When we tailor our approach to suit our own particular challenges and habits, we're far more likely to be able to fashion the order we desire. *Outer Order, Inner Calm* isn't a book about how to clean a house or an office; it's a book about how to boost happiness by creating the outer order that fosters inner calm.

Step by step — as part of our ordinary routine, without spending a lot of time, energy, or money — we can create the orderly surroundings that help us to live happier, healthier, more productive, and more creative lives.

Whenever you read this, and wherever you are, you're in the right place to begin.

■ ■ ■ ■

1
Make Choices

■ ■ ■ ■

If you want a golden rule that will fit
everybody, this is it: Have nothing in your
houses that you do not know to be useful,
or believe to be beautiful.

WILLIAM MORRIS

Clearing clutter is a big challenge. Why?
One reason is that the process requires
us to make taxing choices about what to
keep, what to discard, and why.

Often, to make those choices, we must
confront the reason that we've accumulated
that clutter in the first place. Do any of
these explanations sound familiar?

This thing is so useful that someday I'll
find a way to use it.

I could get this thing fixed or altered.

Life's too short to spend my time dealing
with this thing.

This thing was a gift, so I need to keep it
out of respect for the giver.

This thing hasn't been used up yet.

Just wait, someday this thing will be a collector's item!

I never had this thing as a child, so I want to have it as an adult.

The more things I keep, the more I will leave my family one day.

This thing reminds me of someone I love.

If I deal with this thing now — if I make my bed or wash this dish — I'll just have to deal with it all over again tomorrow.

I'm more creative with all these things around me.

I can't deal with this thing until everyone around me agrees about what we should do with it.

Someday, I might need this thing.

I don't have the space to put away this thing properly.

When I have time, I could do a cool project with this thing.

Going through my things stirs up my emotions and I can't handle that right now.

Everyone I know has this thing, so I should have one, too.

I don't have the time or the energy to decide what to do with this thing.

If I get rid of this thing, and other things, my home or office will feel sterile and stripped.

I've had this thing for so long; I can't get rid of it now.

I forgot about that thing! I didn't even realize it was there.

This thing will feel lonely or abandoned if I get rid of it.

I'll definitely use this thing as soon as I change my life in a major way. I'll get a puppy. I'll lose thirty pounds. I'll form a band.

I don't know where to put this thing, so I'll just put it . . . here.

I have to leave this thing out where I can see it so that I remember to deal with it.

It's exhausting to make decisions; nevertheless, the crucial first step in creating outer order is to figure out what stays and what goes.

Creating outer order becomes far easier when there's less clutter to manage, so it's worth the effort to sort through our possessions. At the same time, it's important to remember that outer order isn't simply a matter of having less or having more; it's a matter of wanting what we have.

Make choices.

PREPARE YOURSELF.

Clearing clutter is exhausting because it requires us to make choices — and making choices is *hard.* It takes intellectual energy as well as emotional energy.

For this reason, clutter-clearing (like everything else in life) is easier when you're well rested, not hungry, and not rushed, and, if necessary, fortified with plenty of caffeine.

For a major clutter-clearing, you may want to recruit a companion to help you make decisions and deal with the grunt work of sorting, moving, packing, and tossing.

Also, proper supplies make the work easier to do. Ziploc bags, garbage bags, labels, storage and recycling bins, plastic gloves, cleaning supplies, a stepladder, a flashlight, a permanent marker, a pair of scissors, boxes, packing tape, a box cutter, manila folders, and paper and a pen may come in handy.

CONSIDER THE THREE BIG QUESTIONS OF CLUTTER.

When trying to decide the fate of a possession, ask yourself:

Do I need it?

Do I love it?

Do I use it?

Sometimes, you use something that you don't love or you need something even though you use it only once every five years. Or perhaps you love something that you never use. That's okay — just because something isn't *being used* doesn't mean it's *useless.*

But if you don't need it, love it, or use it, you should probably get rid of it.

For any possession that passes this test, ask one additional question:

Where does it belong?

Every item should have a specific home.

NEVER LABEL ANYTHING "MISCELLANEOUS."

And don't use a term that's a synonym for "miscellaneous."

I once created a file called ACTIVE USEFUL DOCUMENTS and then never looked in it again.

IDENTIFY YOUR BENEFICIARIES.

It's much easier to let go of unneeded items when we can envision others getting good use from them, so identify people and organizations who will appreciate your contributions.

I found it much easier to clear clutter once I identified:

- an organization that accepts toys
- an organization that accepts books
- an organization that accepts clothes
- a soup kitchen that accepts any unopened packages of food
- a drugstore that safely disposes of unused prescription medications
- a young family who needs children's furniture
- a child who loves dolls and stuffed animals

We had a big pile of board games and puzzles that we no longer used. It occurred to me to ask if my daughter's summer camp would like them. The camp directors were pleased to get these activities for rainy days, and I was gratified to know that these items would be getting such hard use.

DONATE QUICKLY.

When we can't make good use of our possessions, it's time to get those things into the hands of people who will benefit from them.

However, giveaways can quickly accumulate and become a source of clutter themselves. Create a system for moving things out of your house before too much time passes; if you don't, those boxes and bags may take root in their temporary holding spots and stay there for months.

Ask Yourself, "Do I Need More than One?"

As you're clearing clutter, if you discover that you have more than one of an item, ask yourself, "Do I need more than *one*?"

While it can be helpful to have more than one phone charger and more than one pair of scissors, you probably don't need two flour sifters or three pen cups on your desk.

Weirdly, it's often easier to keep track of *one* than of multiples. When I have only one pair of sunglasses, I can always find them. When I have more than one pair, I get careless.

MEMENTOS SHOULD BE CAREFULLY CURATED AND, IF POSSIBLE, SMALL IN SIZE.

I'm a big believer in keeping things for sentimental reasons; remembering happy times in the past gives us a big happiness boost in the present. It's important, though, to think carefully about the things we choose to keep.

Those sweaters you wore in high school — could you keep one sweater instead of five? Or could you take a photo of them? Your grandfather's desk — could you keep his pipe instead? The finger paintings your son brought home from preschool — could you frame your favorite masterpiece to hang on the wall and toss the rest?

The same is true at work. It's easy for a desk to get crowded with trinkets, mementos, and photos that take up a lot of space without providing much value.

Curation matters. Usually (perhaps paradoxically) having *fewer* mementos allows us to hold on to more memories than having *many* mementos does, because these keepsakes have been carefully chosen and we're less overwhelmed by the sheer volume.

Choose a few items that are truly exceptional, and clear out everything else. Find ways to hold on to memories without accumulating mounds of stuff.

Oh! Old rubbish! Old letters, old clothes, old objects that one does not want to throw away. How well nature has understood that, every year, she must change her leaves, her flowers, her fruit and her vegetables, and make manure out of the mementoes of her year!

JULES RENARD

BEWARE OF THE "EASY TO BUY, HARD TO USE" TRAP.

Some items are very easy and satisfying to buy — but then are hard to use.

Gadgets, cookbooks, tech solutions, exercise equipment. . . . They hold great promise, but only if we put them to proper use. And often that takes effort.

Do I really want to figure out how to set up that sleek new device? Am I really going to have the kind of party where I'd use those linen napkins? Am I really committed to using a treadmill? How often do I write a letter on nice stationery?

When deciding what to buy, remember that some things are easy to buy — but then we have to *use* them. If they're not used, they don't enhance our lives; they just contribute to guilt and clutter.

ALLOW TECHNOLOGY TO CLEAR CLUTTER.

Often we hang on to possessions that have been replaced by technology.

Do you consult the print manuals for your devices or appliances — or do you just look up the information online?

Do you maintain a library of books, DVDs, or CDs even though you don't use them anymore?

Do you have a fax machine, even though you never send or receive faxes?

Maybe you still need an alarm clock, calculator, scanner, dictionary, thesaurus, etiquette guide, maps, or copier — but perhaps you use a tech solution instead, so you don't need to keep those things.

If you have the current version of an item, don't keep the outdated version. If you use a new Keurig to make your coffee every day, you don't need your French press.

Unless you actually use these items, there's no need to hang on to them any longer. (Though it does seem like a sacrilege not to own a physical copy of a dictionary.)

DON'T AIM FOR "MINIMALISM."

Outer order isn't a matter of having less or having more; it's a matter of wanting what we have.

For some people, owning a minimal amount of possessions makes them feel freer and happier. That's absolutely true. But it's not true for everyone.

Declaring that we'd all be happier with less (or with more) is like saying that every movie should be 120 minutes long. Every movie has a right length, and people differ in the number of possessions, and the types of possessions, with which they can meaningfully engage. One person is happy with a bare shelf that holds a single vase; another is happy with a shelf lined with books, photographs, and mementos. We must decide what's right for *us*.

Rather than striving for a particular level of possessions — minimal or otherwise — it's helpful to think about getting rid of what's *superfluous*. Even people who prefer to own many possessions enjoy their surroundings more when they've purged everything that's not needed, used, or loved.

CONSIDER THIS CHECKLIST FOR A CLOTHES CLOSET.

Take stock of the items in your closet. As you pull out each garment, ask:

- Does it currently fit?
- Do you actually wear it?
- Do you love it, or if not, is it truly useful?
- Even if you love it, is it in such bad shape that you ought to get rid of it? I struggle with this.
- How many interchangeable items do you own? If you have five pairs of khaki pants, you're not likely to wear your two least favorite pairs.
- Is it uncomfortable?
- Have you worn it five times or fewer? It's the rare item that's worth keeping, even if it's almost never been worn.
- Do you worry that it's out of fashion? If you think it might be, it probably is.
- Can it only be worn in a limited way? Like a shirt that's stained so it can only be worn under a sweater, or shoes that almost never work.
- If you're keeping an item only because

44

it was a gift, does the giver know that you have it? If you don't need to make a show of using it, you don't need to keep it.

■ Does it work with other clothes that you have, or would you need to buy new items to make use of it?

■ Do you keep this item merely to fill a category? If you never wear something, you don't need it. You don't need any turtlenecks if you hate to wear turtlenecks.

■ Does it fill a need that no longer exists? This can be hard to admit, so press yourself.

■ Does it need to be altered before you can wear it? If so, get it altered or get rid of it.

- Do you describe an item of clothing by saying, "I would wear that" or "I have worn that"? These phrases suggest that you don't actually wear it.
- Does your active closet hold clothes that you're keeping for sentimental reasons or for wearing to a costume party? If so, store those items elsewhere. And be choosy; only save things that really deserve it.
- Is a beloved item still flattering but not in top condition? You might "demote" it to more casual use. A sweater can go from a go-out-to-dinner sweater to a hang-around-the-house sweater.

Life is barren enough surely with all her trappings; let us therefore be cautious how we strip her.

SAMUEL JOHNSON

USE A PHOTOGRAPH TO EVALUATE CLUTTER.

At home or at work, if you're having trouble getting started, try taking photos of an area and evaluating what you see.

Somehow, a photograph helps us to see a space with fresh eyes. It changes our perspective and gives us a measure of detachment that can help us decide what items should stay and what need to go.

If someone argues against the need to clear clutter, try showing that person a photo of the space. The area may feel very comfortable — but the objective eye of the camera may help a person recognize that it needs to be cleared out.

Then, once you've cleared the space, take photos of it so that you can compare before and after images. It's a big morale booster to see visual proof of what you've accomplished.

BEWARE OF THE
"SOMEDAY, SOMEONE" RATIONALE.

Sometimes we keep an item because we imagine that "someday, someone will want this."

Ask yourself: How likely is it that someday, someone will want this item?

At home, if something has a very specific use, is in poor condition, is dated, is of sentimental value, is bulky, requires a very particular decorative environment, or needs a lot of upkeep, it's unlikely that it will be used. Someday, someone is likely to throw out that giant aquarium, four-poster bed, damaged bicycle, stuffed animal, or bread-maker from ten years ago.

At work, if an item is obsolete (a catalog from two seasons ago, a desk calendar from last year, outdated business cards), is broken, or belongs to a person who no longer works there, it's unlikely that someday, someone will want it.

PROTECT YOUR PRIME REAL ESTATE.

When bringing order to our surroundings, it's important to consider the value of the real estate.

For instance, a desk is extremely valuable real estate; be very selective about what's on the surface of a work desk, as well as in any shelves, drawers, or cabinets that are within easy reach. Unless you're consulting a book every day, don't leave it on your desk. If you have three boxes of your favorite brand of pen, don't store them in your top drawer.

It's absolutely true that some people find that unexpected juxtapositions spark their creativity, and some people know exactly where to find anything in the pile on their desk. But even for them, work is easier when prime real estate is reserved for the most useful materials.

MOVE CLUTTER OUT OF CONTEXT.
When we see objects settled into a particular place over time, it becomes hard to imagine where else they might go.

So put your clutter into a new context. Pick up items, gather them in a box, and carry the box to a well-ordered room. Once you detach things from their settled places, it's much easier to decide what to do with them.

MOST DECISIONS DON'T REQUIRE EXTENSIVE RESEARCH.
In many situations, we don't need to make a perfect choice but just a good-enough choice.

THREE STRIKES AND YOU'RE OUT.

My father once told me, "People are very reluctant to make a change, so when I started thinking that it might be time to switch jobs, I knew I probably should've switched jobs six months ago."

Along the same lines, people are reluctant to relinquish their possessions, so if I think that it might be time to discard an item, I probably should've done so already — especially if that thought occurs to me more than once.

Now, if three times the thought has occurred to me, "I wonder if I should get rid of that," I get rid of it.

Should I give away that broken tissue box in the shape of old books or keep it?

Should I shred those old credit card statements or retain them?

Should I donate those glass vases or hang on to them?

Three strikes and you're out.

Ask Yourself, "When Was the Last Time I Used This Possession?"

Some things are worth keeping even if they're used only rarely: a good set of binoculars, a sled, formal wear, a box of matches, a cookie baking sheet, a can opener, and power adapters for travel.

But many things are used regularly — or not at all. Either you often use that white-noise generator, bowl for loose change, or electric toothbrush, or you never use it.

If you're not using it, get it into the hands of someone who *will* use it.

BEWARE OF THE "ENDOWMENT EFFECT."

Before you accept something for free or take advantage of a great deal, decide: Do I really *need* this thing? Do I *love* it?

Keep in mind that because of the "endowment effect," we value things more once we own them. Once that thing enters your home, it will be tough to get it out again. A mug, a hand-me-down toy, the lamp from your mother-in-law — if you don't need it, don't take it. If you never possess an item, you don't have to store it, dust it, find it, or figure out how to give it away.

When clearing clutter, one way to fight the endowment effect is to ask, "If I didn't already own this possession, would I buy it?"

If not, why keep it?

ABANDON A PROJECT.

One source of clutter in our homes, and a significant drain on our energy, is the uncomfortable presence of unfinished projects.

Whenever we see evidence of an unfinished project, we get a jolt of annoyance or guilt: "I should finish that," "I need to deal with that," "When am I going to find the time to get that done?"

These projects take many forms: knitting experiments, gardening plans, half-built Lego castles, binders full of untried recipes, woodworking projects, giant puzzles.

Unfinished projects are irritating in themselves, and they also contribute to clutter, because we often leave them out in the open, as a reminder to finish them.

Push yourself to finish an unfinished project or call an end to it. The easiest way to complete a project is to abandon it. Get that stuff off your shelf and off your conscience.

CONSIDER THE X FACTOR.

If you can't decide whether to keep an item of clothing, ask yourself, "If I ran into my ex on the street, would I be happy if I were wearing this?" Often, the answer will give you a good clue.

Beware of the "Duration Effect."

In my own life, I've noticed a phenomenon that's related to the endowment effect — what I think of as the "duration effect."

The longer I own a possession, the more precious it becomes, even if it has never been particularly valued.

We have an ugly, badly designed pair of scissors, but my husband got them as a high school graduation gift — how can we get rid of the scissors now?

This phenomenon is strongest with any possession related to my children. My daughters never played with that china tea set, but now that we've had it for fifteen years, how can we give it away?

Because of the duration effect, I try to hurry unwanted things out the door. The longer I keep them, the harder it is to let them go.

Beware of Conference Swag, Office Freebies, and Promotional Giveaways.

Yes, I went to that conference, and I received a branded mug, a T-shirt, a metal water-bottle, a journal and pen, and an eraser in the shape of a cow. But if I don't have a clear plan to use these things, they're clutter.

The best way to deal with clutter is never to accept these freebies in the first place. Something free can end up costing a lot of time, energy, and space.

Forecast the Future.

Imagine that it's far in the future and your relatives have arrived to clean out your house. What items will they want and what items will they give away, toss, or recycle? You can make their job in the future easier by dealing with your possessions now, instead of foisting that job on them.

ASK YOURSELF, "IS THIS POSSESSION MOVING AROUND?"

Many things, if well used, move around. Clothes come out of their drawers, go to the laundry, return to their place. Books circulate around the house. Dishes come out of the cabinets, get dirty, get clean. For these kinds of possessions, staying in one place for a long time is a clue that they may be clutter.

And are there whole rooms, whole closets, entire filing cabinets, or sets of shelves where nothing comes or goes? These areas begin to feel stale and stagnant, and if nothing they hold ever moves around, they should probably be cleared out.

Don't Get Organized.

When you're facing a desk covered in papers, or a closet bursting with clothes, or countertops littered with piles of random objects, don't say to yourself, "I need to get organized." No!

Your first instinct should be to *get rid* of stuff. If you don't own it, you don't have to organize it.

Beware of "Storing" Things.

For some things — holiday decorations, seasonal clothes, vacation gear — storage makes sense. You put these things away, and when you need them, you get them out again.

But in many cases, storing a possession is just a way to delay deciding what to do with it. It's tempting just to "collect and neglect" — that is, dump something in the attic or the basement rather than figure out whether and how to toss, recycle, or give it away. The U.S. Department of Energy estimates that 25 percent of people who have two-car garages don't park their cars inside because that space is used for storage.

In the long run, you'll be happier if you don't put much into "storage." Before you squirrel something away, ask yourself, "*Why* am I keeping this?" Realistically, are you going to reread your old college textbooks?

Toss Unnecessary Papers.

Paperwork is one of the toughest forms of clutter to vanquish. Getting rid of old papers is less satisfying than cleaning out a closet or a desk drawer, and it's often much more anxiety-provoking.

To decide what to keep and what to toss, ask:

- Do you actually need this piece of paper or receipt? What specific use does it serve?
- Have you ever used it?
- How easy would it be to replace it if you needed it? Except for items like old letters and journals, most things can be replaced.
- Will it quickly become dated — like travel or shopping information?
- Does the internet mean that it's no longer necessary? For instance, the instruction manuals for most appliances are now online.
- What's the consequence of not having it if you do need it?
- Was it once necessary but is now related to a part of your life that's over?

- Could you scan it, so that you have a copy if you need it?
- At work, does someone else have a copy of it?
- Have you verified your assumptions? For instance, when you took your current position, your coworker told you, "I always keep these receipts," so you assumed that you need to keep them, too. But maybe you don't.

One of the Biggest Wastes of Time Is Doing Something Well That Didn't Need to Be Done *at All.*

I got an email from a teacher who complained about how much time she'd spent shredding old lesson plans and student essays.

Why do those papers need to be shredded *at all*?

My sister had accumulated a huge mound of statements and receipts. She wanted to buy a file box to store everything away neatly, but she realized that she'd never needed the papers in the past and that it wouldn't be hard to get copies if she ever did need them. So she tossed all of it.

She didn't need to organize those papers *at all*.

MAKE A MOCK MOVE.

Moving is a great time to clear clutter. Often, when we must go to the trouble to pack up something, we realize that we don't want it anymore.

Take advantage of this phenomenon by doing a mock move. Walk through your rooms, look at what you have, and ask yourself, "If I were moving, would I bother to wrap this in bubble wrap and stick it in a box? Or would I chuck it or give it away?" You may decide not to pack that battered Monopoly game, or the giant ceramic serpent that your daughter made in second grade, or the rice cooker that you've used only once.

So don't wait for a real move. Make your home nicer by tossing, recycling, or donating these items *now*.

CLEAR CLUTTER *BEFORE* YOU MOVE, NOT *AFTER* YOU MOVE.

Moving from one house to another is a stressful, busy time, and it can be tempting to think, I'll just pack everything and sort through it at the other end.

Try to do your sorting before you move. First, you'll save the expense of moving something that you'll eventually just toss or give away. Also, you want to outfit your pristine new home only with the things that you truly need, use, or want. Don't fill it — even temporarily — with useless or un-wanted items.

WHEN IN DOUBT, THROW IT OUT!
OR RECYCLE IT OR GIVE IT AWAY.

ESCAPE FROM CLUTTER LIMBO.

Sometimes, clutter is caused by uncertainty. That toy might be broken or maybe it just needs a new battery. The label-maker might be defective or maybe I didn't push the correct button. This CD might be permanently scratched or maybe it would work if I wiped it off. Did I stop reading this novel, fifty pages in, because I didn't like it or because I just misplaced it?

Move objects out of clutter limbo by taking the steps needed to decide their fate.

Confront Deep Clutter.

There's clutter and then there's *deep clutter.*

Deep clutter is easy to ignore. In deep clutter, items are well organized and put away neatly, and to the inattentive glance, everything looks great — but, in fact, these things are clutter because they aren't used, needed, or loved.

For a long time, I maintained a big notebook with plastic sleeves that held business cards. I'd taken great satisfaction in how perfectly the business cards fit into their slots and how nicely the notebook fit on my shelf.

Then one day I realized that I hadn't consulted a single business card in the past two years. The notebook and the cards were pure clutter. I cleared out the notebook and gave it away.

After we've eliminated the visible and annoying layer of clutter that lies on the surface of life, we can turn our attention to the deep clutter that weighs us down unnoticed.

CLEAR ANY OFF-SITE STORAGE UNITS.

Once you've stashed items in an off-site unit, it's easy to forget about them. But you're paying to store them, month after month after month.

Do you even know what's inside your storage unit?

Visit your unit and make tough choices. If you never need or want these things, why are you keeping them?

FIGHT WASTE BY NOT ACQUIRING.

Many people have trouble clearing clutter because they hate the idea that they're adding more junk to the landfill and putting more trash into the world. But once we own something, that object exists, whether it's in the basement or at the dump.

If this is an issue for you — and even if it's not — fight waste by not acquiring that item in the first place.

DON'T FOIST YOUR CLUTTER ON OTHER PEOPLE.

Getting rid of things can be tough. One unhelpful strategy? To push our stuff onto other people.

Sometimes we press people to accept our things to relieve our own bad feelings: We feel guilty because we spent money on an item that we never used or because we'd like to replace a perfectly serviceable item with something new. To make ourselves feel better about this wastefulness, we push our possessions onto other people — who may or may not actually want them. We use generosity to disguise our true motives.

I've told myself, "I never wore this shirt, but I'll give it to my daughter, and she can wear it" or "I never found a way to use this platter, so I'll give it to my sister." If these recipients really want to have these things, that's wonderful, but I shouldn't press them to be the receivers of my discards to avoid the prick of conscience.

They always say time changes things,
but you actually have to change them
yourself.

ANDY WARHOL

■ ■ ■ ■

2
CREATE ORDER

■ ■ ■ ■

To live in perpetual want of little things
is a state, not indeed of torture, but of
constant vexation.

SAMUEL JOHNSON

Once we've made the key choices about the fate of our possessions, we can begin to establish order.

Imposing order is difficult, but it's also very satisfying to organize, to repair, to put things into their proper places, and to bring life to overlooked areas.

For most people, it's deeply calming to see outer order emerge. Perhaps it's the tangible sense of control, or the relief from visual noise, or the release from guilt and frustration. Creating order — even with things as mundane as socks or supplies — gives a disproportionate boost of energy and cheer. There's so much we can't control, but we can control our stuff.

Create order.

FIX YOUR "BROKEN WINDOWS."

The "broken windows" theory of policing holds that when a community tolerates minor examples of disorder and petty crime, such as broken windows, graffiti, turnstile jumping, or drinking in public, serious crimes are more likely to ensue.

As a law-enforcement theory, it's controversial, but whether or not it's true on a citywide level, I think it's true on a personal level. When our environment is disorderly, it's easier for our behavior to become disorderly.

Some common personal broken windows include:

- unsorted mail and unanswered bills
- messy stacks of newspapers
- shoes in odd places
- no toilet paper
- cluttered counters
- dirty dishes scattered in every room
- piles of laundry or trash
- an unmade bed

It's true that a pile of unsorted mail isn't a big deal. Nevertheless, small instances of order make us feel more in control — and happier.

Beware of "Clutter Magnets."

In just about everyone's house or office, certain areas become "clutter magnets." When I was growing up, it was our dining room table. Nowadays, it's the top of the chest of drawers in the hallway. Also a certain chair in the bedroom. And the counter in my home office. Plus the kitchen table, of course. And I have a tendency to use the bedroom "floordrobe."

Now, every night, I make a real effort to clear those areas. Why? Clutter attracts clutter, so once clutter begins to accumulate, an area tends to get worse and worse.

Get in the habit of clearing clutter magnets regularly. That way, the mounds can never grow too high.

REMEMBER:
IF YOU CAN'T RETRIEVE IT,
YOU WON'T USE IT.

Try to keep things stored within easy reach.

In general, it's more useful to think about *accessibility* than to think about *storage*. If you want to store something but don't care if it's accessible — well, that's a clue that you may not need to keep that item at all.

STOP SEARCHING.

Most of us have one item that somehow we can never find. We spend a lot of time and energy searching for our keys, sunglasses, phone charger, work badge, current book, and so on.

Identify your problem object and then find a way to solve the search problem.

Can't find your keys? Put a hook in your front hall and always put your keys on that hook. Can't find your phone charger once you get to work? Splurge to buy a few charging cords and place them in convenient spots — and never unplug them. Can't find a pen? Buy a bag of pens and put a few in every drawer.

With a little thoughtful effort, we can save ourselves time and spare ourselves frustration.

DON'T WAIT TO
START CREATING ORDER.

At any age, decluttering a house can feel like an overwhelming prospect, and as we get older, it becomes even tougher to do a big sweep. It takes a lot of energy, time, physical strength, and taxing decision-making — plus, it's emotionally draining.

So if your attic, basement, garage, guest room, or office needs to be tackled, don't put off the task too long.

In fact, David Ekerdt, professor of sociology and gerontology, observed that after age fifty, the chances that a person will divest himself or herself of possessions diminishes with each decade.

This can be a real problem, for you and for others. Some people can't move to a new place because they can't face clearing out their current house, and so that burden falls to others.

Do it *now.* Waiting will make it harder, not easier.

SOAP AND WATER REMOVES MOST STAINS.

Usually, we don't need highly specialized cleaning products to deal with common problems.

CHOOSE A "FLAVOR OF THE MONTH."

To make clutter-clearing more fun, choose a theme for the month and focus on the objects in that theme. This approach is arbitrary, but that's one reason that it's effective: it helps us to see our environment in a new, playful way.

Possible themes? Books, clothes, toys, office supplies, kitchen equipment, or bathroom products.

BEWARE OF BUYING SOUVENIRS.
These items may seem wonderful when you're visiting new places, but will you really want to have them on your shelves when you get home?

If you do love to buy travel souvenirs, consider acquiring items that are small, easy to display or use, and yet are good at conjuring memories, such as Christmas tree ornaments, cooking spices, charms for a charm bracelet, postcards.

THINGS OFTEN GET MESSIER BEFORE THEY GET TIDIER.
Sometimes, it can be discouraging to clear clutter, because the process itself generates so much disorder.

It's worth it.

IDENTIFY THE PROBLEM.

Make your workspace more convenient and orderly by taking the time to identify a specific problem.

Is your coat or sweater always in your way? Get a coatrack, use the common closet, or get a hook.

Are you constantly getting tangled in your headphones? Get a desk headphone hanger.

Do you constantly misplace paper with important information? Use a corkboard, take notes in a single notebook, create an in-box for "current vital info," use a vertical file holder to keep papers organized yet within reach.

Many problems have simple solutions — once we take a moment to identify them.

In Active Areas,
Strive to Keep Surfaces Bare.

Put away kitchen appliances you don't use every day; don't cram stuff onto every inch of your desk. Some people thrive in abundance and overflow, but even for them it's helpful to have some clear areas for active work.

DECLARE A
CLUTTER AMNESTY DAY.

Often, we feel guilty for spending too much money on possessions that we didn't really need. And we feel guilty for buying possessions that we've never used at all. And we feel guilty about adding our forsaken possessions to the junk heaps of the world.

Because of that guilt, we hang on to possessions even when we don't want, use, or love them.

Declare a Clutter Amnesty Day. All guilt is absolved. All mistakes are forgiven. Clear that clutter.

The fact is, done is done. Recycle all the unread magazines and articles. Give away unworn clothes, dusty dishes, and abandoned equipment. Declare an end to unfinished projects. Get rid of that single mitten. Then start afresh.

Set all things in their own
peculiar place,
And know that Order is
the greatest Grace.

JOHN DRYDEN

CREATE A "TECH SACK."

Gather any tech items you often use — such as a power cord, wall adapter, headphones, headphone adapter, external power supply — and create a "tech sack" that you can store in a drawer or throw into your briefcase, backpack, purse, or luggage.

BE A TOURIST IN YOUR OWN HOME.

Visit every place in your home or office. See what's inside every cabinet, drawer, closet, and crawl space. Don't feel pressure to deal with it, just look.

When I went on my tour of my apartment, I found troves of plastic cups, thumbtacks, and cotton balls.

Most of us have lots of overlooked areas, where stuff has been stored and forgotten for years. No matter how useful an item might prove to be, if we don't know we possess it, we can't use it.

BATTLE YOUR DUNGEONS.

Most of us have dungeonlike areas in our surroundings — places that seem dank, dirty, neglected, even haunted.

That's unpleasant, so take steps now to eliminate this nastiness. Make sure that no area in your home smells bad, feels dirty, or seems abandoned.

Deal with anything that's sticky, moldy, or musty, whether it's an old jar of honey, a cosmetics bottle streaked with foundation, an oily toolbox, a mildewed shower curtain, a bag of nuts that smells stale, or a laundry-room floor covered with a layer of soap.

If possible, figure out why an area might be damp or crumbling or unstable, and fix it.

In particular, pets can be a source of nastiness: stinky kitty litter, masses of dog hair, smelly aquarium water, old carpets, open bags of food.

These disagreeable and neglected areas weigh us down, so by transforming them, we make the experience of our homes more pleasant.

Brass shines
with constant usage,
a beautiful dress
needs wearing;
leave a house empty,
it rots.

OVID

ASSIGN EACH DAY ITS OWN TASK.

I love the Little House books of Laura Ingalls Wilder. As a child reading *Little House in the Big Woods,* I was fascinated by the idea of assigning a particular household chore to each day of the week. According to Laura,

Wash on Monday,

Iron on Tuesday,

Mend on Wednesday,

Churn on Thursday,

Clean on Friday,

Bake on Saturday,

Rest on Sunday.

This approach can be adapted to the work week, for tasks that are best done periodically. You might . . .

Update spreadsheet on Monday,

Process expense receipts on Tuesday,

Work on monthly report on Wednesday,

Invoice on Thursday,

Make phone calls on Friday.

CREATE A "MYSTERY BOX."

We all accumulate those unattached, important-looking pieces: orphaned cables, random remote-control devices, important-looking screws that appeared on the floor one day, obscure vacuum-cleaner attachments. Collect them all and put them in a box. You'll never use these items, but you'll know they're there. For extra credit, put a date on the box, and if you haven't opened it in a year, throw it away.

SOMETHING THAT CAN BE DONE AT *ANY* TIME IS OFTEN DONE AT *NO* TIME.

Do it now, or decide when you'll do it.

IMAGINE THAT YOU'RE THROWING A PARTY.

Nothing inspires clutter-clearing more than the knowledge that a bunch of people will be visiting.

Even if you're not planning a party now, imagine that you are. Set a date in your mind and ask yourself, "If I'm hosting twelve people for brunch next Sunday, what do I need to do to prepare?"

Really try to put yourself in the host mindset. It's astonishing how many overlooked aspects of your home will spring into your awareness: the fingerprints on the doorjamb, the crumbs in the fridge, the giant toy pile in the corner of the living room.

Along the same lines . . .

IMAGINE YOUR HOME THROUGH THE EYES OF A STRANGER.

Walk around your house as if you were a real estate agent preparing to put it on the market. With a dispassionate eye, evaluate its worth. What aspects might drag down its value and what changes would allow it to command a better price? That junk room could be transformed into an office or an exercise room. Those overloaded shelves could be cleared out. Those burned-out light bulbs could be replaced.

Or imagine that you're someone who's considering paying for a short-term rental of the space. What would you think of those photos on the Airbnb website?

Or imagine that you're the executor of the estate, or a professional organizer, or a house cleaner called in to bid on a big job.

By assuming another identity — a stranger who doesn't have a personal love for our possessions and space — we foster the detachment that makes it easier to create order.

It is by studying little things that we attain the great art of having as little misery and as much happiness as possible.

SAMUEL JOHNSON

IDENTIFY AN EXACT PLACE
FOR EVERYTHING.

Counterintuitively, it's easier — and also more fun — to put things away in an *exact* place rather than a general place.

Life goes more smoothly when you know exactly where to find certain essential possessions. For instance, know where to find your:

passport
flashlight
vegetable peeler
Band-Aids
AA batteries
heating pad
pair of scissors
last year's tax returns
screwdriver
birth certificate
teaspoon measure
packing tape

Added benefit: When things belong in an exact place, it's easier for other people to find them, and it's easier for other people to put things away. Everybody knows that the extension cord belongs on the left side of the closet's third shelf.

GET ORGANIZED — BUT NOT TOO ORGANIZED.

There's great pleasure and value in having a place for everything, but this impulse can become inefficient. Don't get overly specific. If you spend a lot of time alphabetizing your soup cans or setting up fifteen categories for your home library, consider simplifying your approach.

Also, some things simply won't stay organized, so it's not even worth trying; I've spent hours sorting crayons and Lego pieces, only to find them all jumbled up again the next day.

BEWARE THE SIREN CALL OF INVENTIVE STORAGE CONTAINERS.

Perhaps unsurprisingly, it's often the people with the worst clutter problems who have the instinct to run to a store to buy complicated hangers, drawer compartments, and so on.

Don't buy a container until it's absolutely clear that it will help you organize objects that are truly necessary — rather than act as a crutch to move clutter around or to jam more clutter into place.

If you need to buy things to store things, perhaps you have too many things.

Don't spend money on containers for possessions that will be packed away nicely, then utterly forgotten. The right container can be invaluable, but if you get rid of the things you don't need, use, or love, you may not need those containers at all.

PRACTICE *MISE-EN-PLACE.*

Sophisticated cooks talk about *mise-en-place,* which is French for "everything in its place." *Mise-en-place* describes the preparation that's done before the actual cooking starts: gathering ingredients and implements, chopping, measuring, and all the rest.

Mise-en-place means that a cook has everything at the ready, with no need to make a trip to the store or begin a frantic search for a paring knife.

Whenever possible, practice *mise-en-place.* Creating order is easier when we take the time to set up properly. Is your mail situation out of control? Establish a place where you can find your stamps, envelopes, return-address labels, checkbook, and letter opener. As soon as you're ready to act, the materials are ready for your use.

CLEAN AS YOU GO.

Clean as you cook, hang up your clothes right after you put on your pajamas, put files back in the filing cabinet as soon as you've retrieved what you need. If you clean up after yourself along the way, clutter stays far more manageable.

For most people, it's easier to do little tasks as they arise rather than face a giant task at the end.

CREATE A "BOWL OF REQUIREMENT."

In the Harry Potter books, Harry finds a Room of Requirement that magically holds anything a person requires. Inspired by this idea, I now create a "bowl of requirement" every time I travel to a new place.

I find a bowl or a tray and in it I place anything that might be required by me or a member of my family: keys, sunglasses, earbuds, loose change, wallet.

I'd noticed that when traveling, I often misplaced things because I put them down randomly, in an unfamiliar setting. By identifying a place where everything important should go, I've spared myself hours of irritated searching.

CREATE HOLDING BINS.

When people share a space — a couple, a family, roommates in a dorm, officemates — they often have different levels of tolerance for clutter. And this can cause a lot of arguments.

If you crave order more than the other people who share your space, consider creating holding bins for their stuff. Keep these bins somewhere inconspicuous yet convenient, and when you want to create more order, put their out-of-place items in their bins. It's a lot quicker and easier than putting things away in their proper places — especially if you don't know where those things belong.

This way, items are out of the common areas, yet easily found by their owners. If necessary, you can also have an extra bin for items without a clear owner.

KEEP PENS, A NOTEPAD, SCOTCH TAPE, AND A PAIR OF SCISSORS IN EVERY ROOM.

Life is much easier when you have the tools you need right within reach.

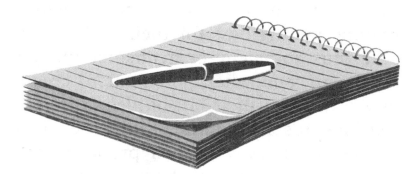

Find a Place for Items That Are Neither Dirty nor Clean.

Many people struggle to manage clothes that are neither fresh from the washing machine nor ready to be laundered: the sweatpants you've worn a few times, the shirt you wore for an afternoon.

When people feel uncomfortable mixing not-dirty clothes with clean ones, they tend to accumulate clothes in odd places. If you feel this way, find a method for handling those in-between clothes. Put hooks for them in your bathroom or closet; set aside a special drawer.

WHAT WE ASSUME WILL BE TEMPORARY OFTEN BECOMES PERMANENT; WHAT WE ASSUME IS PERMANENT OFTEN PROVES TEMPORARY.

Begin the way you want to continue, because temporary often becomes permanent. If members of your family dump their stuff on the floor of the front hallway during the first few weeks you live in your new house, everyone will form a habit that will be hard to change — so work hard to establish desirable habits right from the first day.

On the other hand, what seems permanent often proves temporary. You may think that you'll have a grubby high chair in your kitchen forever, but before you know it, that high chair will be gone.

■ ■ ■ ■

3
KNOW YOURSELF —
AND OTHERS

■ ■ ■ ■

The things that we love
tell us what we are.

THOMAS MERTON

There are no magic, one-size-fits-all
solutions for establishing order; we all
need to do it in the way that's right for *us.*

One person thinks, Out of a spirit of detachment, I can let go of this stuff, because these
things are meaningless. Another person
thinks, Out of a spirit of engagement, I can
let go of this stuff, because a few treasured
items mean more than a pile of things I
can't handle.

We can all learn from one another, but
there's no best way to achieve anything. No
one's right and no one's wrong.

When we know *ourselves,* we can customize our surroundings and our systems to suit ourselves — rather than try to force ourselves to follow someone else's methods. Approached in the proper spirit, clearing clutter becomes an exercise in self-knowledge.

And when we know *others* and how they might see the world in a different way, we can find ways for everyone to thrive.

I have my reasons for wanting to create order, and certain kinds of order matter more to me than others. I don't mind seeing dirty dishes in the sink, but I dislike seeing dog toys scattered across the floor. My husband is just the opposite. Recognizing these differences makes it easier to maintain a household that's pleasant for both of us.

We can curate our spaces to help us show other people (and ourselves) who we are.

Know yourself — and others.

KNOW YOUR PURPOSE.

It's easy to assume that we "should" undertake a particular clutter-clearing task. When we're very clear about *why* we're doing it, it's easier to use our time and energy productively — and also to recognize success.

Ask yourself, "*Why* am I clearing this clutter? What's my purpose?" If you start clearing the garage because you think you "should," you might partly clean it out, get distracted, stop, and never finish. If you think, I'm cleaning the garage because I want to be able to park my car here, so I won't have to scrape snow and ice off my windshield on winter mornings, you're more likely to finish the task. Because your purpose is clear, you're more inclined to keep going, and you'll feel greater satisfaction in completing the job.

On the other hand, if you don't see much purpose in tackling a task, you don't need to worry too much about it. Outer order is something to pursue if it makes you (or someone else) happier; not for its own sake.

ASK YOURSELF, "WHAT ARE MY CLUTTER PEEVES?"

Clutter comes in many forms. Clothes clutter, toy clutter, paper clutter, kitchen clutter, pet clutter, schoolwork clutter, car clutter, counter clutter, laundry clutter . . .

Make the biggest effort to deal with the kind of clutter that bothers you the most.

NO ONE EVER REGRETS HAVING REPLACED A LIGHT BULB.

Go ahead and replace that bulb right now. Without delay is the easiest way. And while you're at it, replace that empty roll of toilet paper as well.

Do You "Treat" Yourself to a Mess?

When we're feeling blue or overwhelmed, it's tempting to indulge in a "treat," but we often try to make ourselves feel *better* by giving ourselves treats that make us feel *worse*. An ice cream sundae, an extra glass of wine, a binge session of TV watching, an expensive splurge, and other such treats give a short-term boost, but then guilt and remorse set in.

One of my favorite unhealthy treats? Telling myself, "I can't keep things orderly, I'm too busy. I deserve a break."

The problem is that, for me and for most of us, the mess just makes us feel worse. Feeling overwhelmed is a reason to try to maintain order, not to abandon order.

Outer order contributes to inner calm.

ARE YOU FURNISHING A
FANTASY IDENTITY?

Maybe you wish you lived a life where a particular object would be useful — a fantasy existence where you'd make good use of hand weights, embroidered hand towels, a briefcase, a guitar, or electric tools.

Or perhaps you want to present a fantasy self to others. You want people to think you're a student of history and foreign policy, or a serious movie buff, so you accumulate the trappings to present that picture of yourself.

It can be painful to admit that we aren't going to use certain possessions — but all that junk just gets in our way. Be honest with yourself and clear those things off your shelves, and you'll have more room for the things that you truly love and use.

Are You Clinging to an Outdated Identity?

Do you still keep all your ski equipment even though you blew out your knee and no longer ski? Sometimes, we're sad to relinquish an identity, so we cling to possessions as a way to insulate ourselves from change.

Do you still subscribe to *The New Yorker,* even though you never read it anymore? Sometimes, we haven't noticed that our identity has evolved and that items once useful or appealing no longer suit us.

Do you still keep all your work suits, even though you never go to an office these days? Sometimes, because we've devoted a lot of time, effort, or expense to a period of our lives, we hang on to the things associated with it.

A few beloved, well-chosen mementos can help us recall old times, but keeping too much stuff keeps us stuck in the past and cramps our ability to embrace the present.

BEWARE OF FAKE-WORK AND MAKE-WORK.

Creating outer order is a worthy aim, but we want to avoid making unnecessary work for ourselves.

Looking up information that's not needed, spending a lot of time perfecting the format of a casual report, putting labels on a notebook that doesn't need labels . . . order and organization are valuable when they help us work more easily and efficiently, but we should be wary of allowing them to become an end in themselves.

Just because we're *busy* doesn't mean we're being *productive.* Working is one of the most dangerous forms of procrastination.

IS YOUR CLUTTER *BACKWARD-LOOKING* OR *FORWARD-LOOKING*?

People with backward-looking clutter keep items as reminders of the past. "Years ago, we had so much fun building this castle out of Popsicle sticks."

People with forward-looking clutter keep items as preparation for the future. "One day, I might need this oversize glass jar."

When we recognize the patterns in the possessions we cling to, we can more easily decide what to keep.

STAY CURRENT WITH A CHILD'S INTERESTS.

Kids are often given gifts they don't want.

Sometimes parents are eager to promote a passion, such as chess, water painting, or guitar. So they buy lots of equipment and supplies, even after the child has lost interest.

Sometimes a relative or a family friend buys things that the child has outgrown — like the godparent who keeps sending dinosaur-themed gifts long after the child has outgrown the dinosaur phase.

Remember how quickly children's interests and desires change.

Do You Take a *Practical View* or a *Mystical View* Toward Your Possessions?

Some people see their possessions as inanimate objects to be sorted and stored.

Others take a more mystical view. For them, possessions have spirits of their own: those socks might feel uncomfortable crowded into a drawer; that vase might feel lonely on its shelf; the dinner plates must be rotated so that none feels indignant at being ignored; that suitcase is a loyal companion.

As a child, it seemed to me that the pillows decorating my bed got their feelings hurt if they weren't displayed properly.

If you take a more mystical view, it may be harder to relinquish possessions. When it's time, thank them for their service, acknowledge the contribution they've made to your life, and allow them to pass to the next stage of their existence.

Every January 1, a friend cleans her fridge *totally* — the leftovers, the jars of mustard, the pickles, everything. I would never do something so wasteful, but I absolutely understand the impulse to start the year with fresh, new recruits, with nothing tired from its service.

MIND YOUR OWN BUSINESS.
Sometimes, we're annoyed by other people's clutter, even when it doesn't affect us. We say, "Clean out your messy backpack," "Don't pack for a business trip at the last minute," "Alphabetize your bookshelf," or "Clean up your desk."

But if a person's clutter affects only that person, don't interfere unless asked. Different people view clutter in different ways, and we can preserve our time, energy, and patience by not worrying needlessly about other people.

OFFICE SUPPLIES AREN'T USEFUL IF THEY AREN'T USED.

For many of us, especially at work, it feels easier and safer to keep something rather than to shred, recycle, donate, toss, or leave it in the supply closet.

Also, as a job and the world evolve, it's easy to accumulate tools, resources, and files related to work that we no longer do. When I was clearing out my home office, I realized that for years, I've had a digital voice recorder that I've never once used (and I never will use, because if I do need to make a recording, I'll use my smartphone). I put the recorder in my donation box.

It's also easy to acquire supplies that seem useful, but that don't actually get any use, such as a three-hole punch, legal pads, a ruler, or a calculator, or to stockpile items like binder clips, empty three-ring binders, highlighters, or packets of ketchup and salt.

Keep only those items you actually *use.*

ARE YOU IN THE
"SEASON OF STUFF?"

Parents of young children have to deal with a lot of stuff, and that stuff often creates clutter.

Little kids need strollers, high chairs, cribs, car seats, and diaper pails. They often have big toys, like play kitchens or massive block sets. They need specialized equipment for ordinary activities.

If you're irritated by all this clutter, remember, it will pass. Although older children do create a different kind of maddening clutter, their possessions usually take up less space — and eventually those children move out.

I remind myself that the things that annoy me *now* are the things that I'll remember with longing in the future. Although at one time keeping a stroller in the hallway drove me crazy, now I think back with intense nostalgia, Ah, remember those days when we had a baby and a stroller!

The days are long, but the years are short.

ASK YOURSELF, "I'VE INHERITED THIS ITEM, BUT DO I WANT TO KEEP IT?"

When we inherit something, it's very tempting to keep it.

Perhaps this item reminds you of someone you loved. Perhaps this item was important to someone else. And if nothing else, it's free.

But that furniture — that set of china, those tools, those decorative items that don't reflect your taste — if you won't use them, don't keep them.

LEARN FROM YOUR SUCCESSES.

Even if you're surrounded by clutter, is there a place that stays clear? If you're great with mail but bad with clothes perhaps you can find a way to deal with clothes in a way that's more like mail.

Maybe you're messy at home but clutter-free at work, or vice versa. What makes it easier to keep your surroundings in good order in one environment but not in the other?

Or maybe you're drowning in clutter now, but you were clutter-free in the past. What made it easier to stay neat then?

Think about why certain systems help you maintain order, and look for lessons that you can apply elsewhere in your life.

You learn more about a person by living in his house for a week than by years of running into him at social gatherings.

PHILLIP LOPATE

ARE YOU A *COUNTER-FILLER* OR A *COUNTER-CLEARER?*

Do you like to keep items on the counter, out in the open and ready for use, or do you prefer to keep your counters bare, with things hidden away?

On a friend's kitchen counter I spotted, among other things, a pepper mill, a cutting board, a bottle of pain reliever, a spoon rest, and a bagel slicer — all things that I prefer to keep stored out of sight.

There's no right approach, just what makes you comfortable.

Even for people who like to see objects around them, however, this system works better when items aren't piled haphazardly but rather carefully selected and purposefully placed where they can serve their function.

Reconsider Gift-Giving.

Giving gifts is a wonderful tradition, but it can lead to the exchange of possessions that no one really wants.

To make sure that you receive and give items that will actually be used, keep lists of gift ideas for yourself and other people, and encourage people to use wish lists.

Some people agree to follow a holiday rule: Something you want, something you need, something to wear, and something to read.

Many people reach a point where they don't want any more "stuff." If so, give the gift of an experience rather than a possession, by taking them to a restaurant, cooking them a meal, taking them to a performance or an exhibit, paying for exercise sessions for them, volunteering to tackle a necessary chore for them, or the like.

ASK YOURSELF, "DO I CARE?"

Remember, the reason to clear clutter is because, somehow, that clutter is diminishing your happiness.

If you don't care, *don't bother.* I have a friend who has a beautiful, well-organized house except for the entryway — which is crammed with a chaotic mess of shoes, backpacks, sports equipment, and overloaded coat hooks.

She just doesn't care.

ARE YOU A *MARATHONER* OR A *SPRINTER*?

If you're gearing up to clear clutter, what appeals to you more: doing a little bit each day until the job is finished or taking a solid chunk of time and blasting through to completion?

Marathoners prefer to work at a slow and steady clip, and they don't like being pressed against deadlines. A marathoner might decide to tackle clutter for thirty minutes each day, or to clear one shelf or drawer at a time, until all the clutter is gone.

Sprinters prefer to work in bursts of intense effort, and they often welcome the pressure of a deadline. A sprinter might choose to go to the office on a Saturday morning for a massive single effort to clear out a desk, or to invite guests to stay for the next weekend as a way to create clutter-clearing pressure.

There's no right or wrong way to clear clutter.

ARE YOU AN *UPHOLDER,* A *QUESTIONER,* AN *OBLIGER,* OR A *REBEL?*

In my book *The Four Tendencies,* I describe the personality framework that I've devised to explain how people respond differently to expectations. This Four Tendencies framework distinguishes people based on how they respond to *outer expectations* (meet a deadline, answer a request from a friend) and *inner expectations* (start meditating, keep a New Year's resolution).

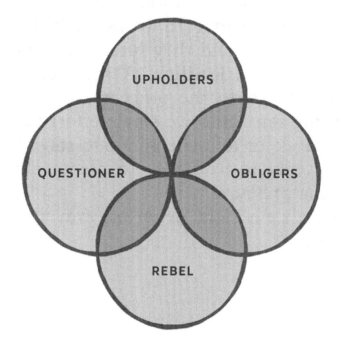

UPHOLDER responds readily to outer and inner expectations.

QUESTIONER questions all expectations; they'll meet an expectation *if* they think it makes sense — essentially, they make all expectations into inner expectations.

OBLIGER meets outer expectations but struggles to meet inner expectations.

REBEL resists all expectations, outer and inner alike.

Your "response to an expectation" may sound slightly obscure, but it turns out to be very important. For instance, when you're trying to clear clutter:

IF YOU'RE AN UPHOLDER: Because Upholders gravitate toward to-do lists, schedules, and planning, if you want to sort through a bunch of office files, slot that task into your calendar.

IF YOU'RE A QUESTIONER: Questioners focus on the reasons for their actions, so remind yourself of the time, space, and serenity you'll gain by clearing clutter. Questioners often raise questions like "Why make the bed if we'll just mess it up again"? The more you see the justifications for your efforts, the more easily you'll follow through.

IF YOU'RE AN OBLIGER: To meet inner expectations, Obligers need outer accountability, so to clear clutter, create accountability. Invite a friend to keep you company; hire a professional organizer; promise someone that you'll deliver your hand-me-downs; invite someone to stay for the weekend; consider it your duty to be a good role model for others; think of how others will benefit from a well-organized, spacious environment; reflect on how your future self will feel; start or join an accountability group.

IF YOU'RE A REBEL: Rebels do what they want to do. Remind yourself that clearing clutter isn't something you should do, or that you must do, or what others expect from you — it's what you want. Instead of keeping a to-do list, keep a "could-do" list of all the things you could do, if you feel like it. Rebels also tend to like a challenge. "My boss thinks that I can't clear these storage shelves in one afternoon. Watch me."

ARE YOU AN *OVERBUYER?*

Some people buy too much, some people buy too little.

You're an **overbuyer** if . . .

- you tend to accumulate large stores of slow-moving items like shampoo or cough medicine.
- you often make a purchase, such as a tool or a tech gadget, with the thought, I'll probably be able to use this.
- you have a long list of stores to visit before you travel.
- you find yourself throwing things away — milk, medicine, even cans of soup — because they've hit their expiration date.
- you buy items with the thought *This will make a great gift!* without having a recipient in mind.

Overbuyers feel stressed because they're hemmed in by stuff. They often don't have enough storage space for everything they've bought, or they can't find what they have. They feel oppressed by the number of errands they believe they need to do and by the waste and clutter often created by their overbuying.

So, overbuyers, think it over before you whip out your wallet! You don't need a ten-year supply of toothpaste.

On the other hand . . .

ARE YOU AN *UNDERBUYER?*

Some people buy too much, some people buy too little.

You're an **underbuyer** if . . .

- you often scramble to buy an item like a winter coat or a bathing suit after the point at which you need it.
- you resist buying things dedicated to very specific uses: suit bags, facial tissue, hand cream, rain boots.
- you often need to come up with a makeshift solution, such as using soap instead of shaving cream, because you don't have what you need.
- you often consider buying an item, then decide, "I'll get this some other time" or "Maybe we don't really need this."

Underbuyers feel stressed because they don't have the things they need. They're often surrounded with things that are shabby, don't really work, or aren't exactly suitable.

Underbuyers — buy what you need without procrastination! Don't wait for the morning of your ski trip to buy ski gloves.

And speaking of underbuyers . . .

140

BEWARE OF UNDERBUYER CLUTTER.
It's easy to understand why overbuyers might struggle with clutter. But because underbuyers dislike buying things, you might assume that they wouldn't have issues with clutter.

In fact, the underbuyer distaste for shopping actually contributes to their clutter. Because they dread the thought of needing an item and being forced to go buy it, they find it very hard to let go of anything, no matter how useless. "I've only used this ice cream maker one time since I got it, but someday I might want to make ice cream, and I'd have to go out and buy an ice cream maker."

The best guide to the future is the past. If you haven't used that thing since you acquired it, it's unlikely you'll start now.

Feeling Blue? Try Cleaning Up.

This strategy won't work for everyone, but some people (like me) find it soothing to clear clutter. The gentle activity, the action of putting things in their proper places, and the visual gratification of seeing order emerge from a mess combine to give a big boost.

Give it a shot. The next time you feel angry, anxious, or unhappy, try establishing some order to your surroundings. You might feel a lot better.

I have a friend who was furious with her father, so she spent the day cleaning out her office. Sorting, tossing, creating space, and organizing helped her to calm down.

Also, if someone else is driving you crazy with a sudden burst of clutter-clearing, remember, that person may be using outer order to deal with anxiety, sorrow, or anger.

Ask "Who Owns This?"

Often, clutter sticks around because it's not clear who owns it — so no one feels authorized to get rid of it.

Sure, there's an odd lotion bottle in the cabinet that you never use, but *someone* in your house bought it. Does that person use it? Or that book, that exercise gear, that cord. To whom do these things belong?

The question of ownership can be a particular problem at the office — those aren't your files and no one seems to know why they've been sitting in the hallway for two years, but how can you throw them away?

If you encounter something that you think is clutter, ask around and find out if anyone wants it. It's surprising how often things go unclaimed.

BEWARE OF THE TRAGEDY OF THE MESSY COMMONS.

When several people use one space and no one person is responsible for keeping order, people tend to become messy and careless.

This pattern can be a particular problem in the office. The sink and counters in the office kitchen, the mail area, and the conference rooms get used by everyone, but not everyone is careful to clean up.

These common areas can cause a lot of strife. In my observation, the best system is officially to assign a particular person the job of maintaining order in each area.

Don't Let the Perfect Be the Enemy of the Good.

Know your capacity — and recognize your limits.

Actually spending ten minutes clearing off one shelf is better than fantasizing about spending a weekend cleaning out the basement.

Actually clearing out most of the clothes you don't wear is better than fantasizing about hiring an expensive closet-design company.

Even if we can't create or maintain perfect order, it's still worth trying to make things *better.*

ARE YOU STORING SECONDHAND CLUTTER?

Sometimes, our houses get packed with things that we're storing for someone else — someone who may not even want those things.

You've been keeping shelves full of your son's old trophies so he can have them when he wants them — but will he ever claim them?

Some friends of mine were asked to store a friend's very large collection of matchbooks while she was transferred overseas for a year. Even though they lived in a very cramped New York City apartment, they agreed to store her collection, which took up valuable space in one of their few closets. She ended up staying abroad for three years, and when she finally returned to New York City, they asked her to retrieve her collection and she said, "Oh, just throw it out. I don't want it."

Be wary about storing items for someone else unless it's very clear that that person values them.

ASK YOURSELF, "DOES THIS MEMENTO ACTUALLY HOLD MEMORIES FOR ME?"

Mementos are possessions meant to remind us of the people, activities, and places we love. But sometimes we hang on to these items even when they're meaningless.

You have a mug with a photo of a team of people with whom you briefly worked ten years ago, but you don't even remember their names now.

You inherited a big box of family photographs, but you don't recognize anyone in the pictures.

Your father gave you his father's fishing rod, but you never met your grandfather and never go fishing.

Don't save mementos that hold no memories for you; don't keep a keepsake unless you value it.

ARE YOU CLUTTER-BLIND? OR ARE YOU DEALING WITH SOMEONE WHO IS?

Very often, people in a couple or in a group have different levels of tolerance for clutter, and the ones with the least tolerance end up doing the most tidying, and the ones with the most tolerance end up doing less.

However, in most cases, the messier ones eventually cave and do some clutter-clearing, too. They also want to be in an environment that is reasonably orderly (though people often disagree about what is "reasonable").

But there are some people who are truly clutter-blind — who don't seem to register clutter *ever.*

If you're clutter-blind yourself, you may be mystified by why other people complain so much about your mess.

If you're dealing with people who are truly clutter-blind, accept that it's very difficult to prod them to contribute to clutter-busting efforts because they neither see nor care about clutter. It just doesn't register in their consciousness.

Realizing that other people see clutter dif-

ferently can help us deal more patiently with
them.

DO YOU STRUGGLE TO GET RID OF POSSESSIONS THAT ONCE GAVE YOU GREAT PLEASURE OR SERVICE?

In *The Theory of Moral Sentiments,* philosopher Adam Smith observed:

> We conceive . . . a sort of gratitude for those inanimated objects, which have been the causes of great, or frequent pleasure to us. The sailor, who, as soon as he got ashore, should mend [build] his fire with the plank upon which he had just escaped from a shipwreck, would seem to be guilty of an unnatural action. We should expect that he would rather preserve it with care and affection, as a monument that was, in some measure, dear to him.

I love this passage, but the old-fashioned language may obscure Smith's thought-provoking point: When some object has done us a great service, we're reluctant to get rid of it.

For instance, I found it hard to say good-bye to my old laptops. They worked so hard for me; we've had so many good times together. But my old laptops were starting to take up a lot of space, so I took a photograph of them as a memento and sent them on their way.

SOME PEOPLE HAVE VERY STRONG VIEWS ABOUT THE RIGHT WAY TO LOAD A DISHWASHER.

Dishwasher loading may be a good area to decide: "This issue matters more to someone I love than it matters to me. Out of love, I'll load the dishwasher according to that person's method, even if I think it's unnecessary, silly, illogical, or a waste of time."

Or if you just can't bring yourself to adopt someone else's crazy method, agree to consult the manual together to decide the "best" way to do it.

MY CLUTTER FEELS DIFFERENT FROM YOUR CLUTTER.

Have you ever noticed that if you're making a noise — clicking a pen, drumming your fingers, humming — the noise doesn't bother you, but when someone else makes that kind of noise, it's very annoying?

It's the same way with stuff. Often, we don't mind or don't even see our *own* clutter, but we're very bothered by *other people's* clutter. A friend told me, "My husband complains about my crumbs on the kitchen counter while he's created a giant mess in the living room."

Keep this phenomenon in mind if someone asks you to clean up an area, even when the disorder doesn't seem bothersome to you — or if someone seems surprised that you've asked him or her to clean up.

STORE THINGS AT THE STORE.
Are you the kind of person who tends to buy items with the thought, This will probably come in handy? Do you buy enormous quantities of common items (tinfoil, paper towels, dental floss) with the thought, I might run out of this, so I'd better stock up? If so, remind yourself, If and when I need this, I can buy it. Maybe I'll never need it, so I'll store it at the store.

**IF YOU WANT HELP,
ASK FOR IT DIRECTLY.**
People respond with more cooperation, and less resentment, to direct suggestions; passive-aggressive comments and loud sighs are more often ignored. Instead of "This place is a mess," try "Please take your school stuff off the kitchen table." Instead of "No one ever helps clean up around here," try "Please unload the dishwasher so we can move the dirty dishes out of the sink."

WAVE YOUR MAGIC WAND.
Imagine that you have a magic wand.

What would you do with a magic room — an extra room that mysteriously appeared in your house?

What would you accomplish with a magic task — a task that got completed overnight with no work from you?

Thinking about what you'd do with magical help can help identify possible changes to make in your life.

For instance, if magic would give you a yoga room, might you find space for a yoga room in your home right now? If magic would clean out the garage, might you delegate or pay someone to do that task for you? That's almost as good as magic.

A true home is the finest ideal of man.
FRANK LLOYD WRIGHT

Don't Expect Praise
or Appreciation.

If you clear clutter with the expectation that other people will appreciate and praise your efforts, you may end up feeling very frustrated.

Some people (such as me) find it easier to clear clutter when they tell themselves, "I'm doing it for myself." Other people find it easier when they tell themselves, "I'm doing this for someone else — for other members of my family, for guests, for strangers."

Either way, don't expect people to react the way you'd like. People aren't always good at saying "Thank you." Or even noticing.

ACCEPT YOURSELF, AND EXPECT MORE FROM YOURSELF.

Or as writer Flannery O'Connor put it, "Accepting oneself does not preclude an attempt to become better."

We can accept ourselves and acknowledge what's true about our nature and habits — and we can also ask ourselves to try harder, in our approach to clearing clutter, and for everything else.

■ ■ ■ ■

4
CULTIVATE
HELPFUL
HABITS

■ ■ ■ ■

A small daily task,
if it be really daily, will
beat the labours of a
spasmodic Hercules.

ANTHONY TROLLOPE

To clear clutter, we must first make choices and create order. Once we've done that, knowing ourselves helps us to recognize what systems and strategies will work for us.

The next step is to build on that knowledge and that foundation, by establishing helpful habits.

Easy, quick, regular habits make it possible to manage possessions before they accumulate into clutter. We often underestimate what we can do in short bits of time — if we follow habits that maintain order. It's far easier to keep up than to catch up, and with the right habits, clutter never accumulates.

True, it's tiresome to worry about clutter and the habits that combat it, but once habits are formed, those behaviors happen automatically. Think about clutter now to forget about clutter later.

Cultivate helpful habits.

Follow the "One-Minute Rule."

Do any task that can be finished in less than one minute, without delay. Hang up a coat, read a letter and toss it, put a document in a file, throw away a pen that doesn't work, put the toothpaste back in the medicine cabinet and close the door.

Because the tasks are so quick, it isn't too hard to follow this rule, and it's amazing how much can get done, in one-minute increments, over the course of a few weeks.

WALKING FROM ROOM TO ROOM? TAKE ONE THING WITH YOU.

Whenever you walk from one room to another room, take one thing with you. You don't have to take this item to its final destination, just move it closer. When you walk out of the kitchen, take your sweater with you. Don't take it all the way to your closet right now, just move it closer to your closet.

Little by little, things begin to move into place.

DON'T PUT THINGS DOWN; PUT THINGS AWAY.

If you hear yourself saying, "I'll put this here and deal with it later," beware!

OPEN ITEMS CAREFULLY.

Most items are designed so that if they're opened as intended, they're both easier to open and easier to close — but when we're impatient or inattentive, we may ignore that and yank an item open.

If you rip open the bag of dog treats, you may not be able to reseal the package. If you rip open the box of Ziploc bags, you may not be able to close the box again easily. If you rip out that toy, you may not be able to store the toy in its original box. On the other hand, if you open the box of tea bags in the way that it's meant to be opened, it will easily close again.

Make it a habit to look for the pull tag or the notch in the envelope. A little extra effort and attention make life easier in the long run.

USE IT UP,
WEAR IT OUT,
MAKE IT WORK,
OR DO WITHOUT.

Beware the Urge to "Procrasticlear."

Sometimes, I get the very strong urge to clear clutter — not from the true desire for outer order, but from the desire to delay work on some unpleasant task.

The crowded shelves in my office had never bothered me, but now that it's time to face a tough assignment, I'm convinced that nothing can possibly get accomplished until I've dealt with those shelves.

It's true that creating outer order can clear our minds, release energy, and help us prepare to tackle big tasks. But we need to be sure that clutter-clearing doesn't become an excuse to postpone work on something that's actually more important.

One way to identify procrasticlearing is to ask yourself: If I'd finished the dreaded task, would I still feel the need to create that outer order? If not, I'm just procrasticlearing.

There's a real difference between helpful preparation and unhelpful procrastination.

FIND ROOM OF ONE'S OWN.

Virginia Woolf famously argued that a writer needs "a room of one's own." And if you're like most people, you probably want room of your own, even if you're not a writer. Do you want some room of your own — and if so, do you have it?

You might not be able to get an *entire* room to yourself, but you can probably claim *some* room — a closet, a desk, a filing cabinet, a corner of the basement, whatever works.

If you share a space with others, you need an area that belongs just to you, one that's ordered and maintained under your sole control.

In that area, you have an expectation of privacy; you can leave out materials related to an ongoing project; you can put things where you want; others can't rearrange your things; and no one can borrow anything without permission.

Keep your "room" free from anything that's not yours. At home, don't allow it to be used as a dump zone for other family members. At work, don't allow coworkers to use it as a storage area or holding place.

A little space can make a big difference.

BE ALERT FOR SIGNS OF CLUTTER-CUMULATION.

Clutter is insidious; it creeps in gradually and often we don't notice it until it has formed an intimidating heap.

Watch out for these signs:

- a closet door that has to be forced to close
- a drawer that won't slide shut
- things stored in double rows, one behind the other
- items jammed into place at an angle
- lids that won't close
- piles that persist for more than a few days on the floor, on a counter, or under a table
- an item situated in a place that's clearly inappropriate (e.g., a printer set up on a living room chair or a baseball glove on an office desk)
- piles that interfere with the normal use of a space (e.g., the dining room table is so crowded with stuff that it can't be used)

- an item that's stored out of proper context (e.g., a box of stationery on the top shelf of a clothes closet)

NOTHING
IS MORE
EXHAUSTING
THAN THE TASK
THAT'S
NEVER STARTED.

MAKE A HABIT OF THE TRAVEL TIDY-UP.

When you're waiting to board an airplane, train, or bus, take a few minutes to clean out your purse, backpack, or briefcase.

It's an easy way to make good use of that transitional time. You don't have much else to do, you're usually sitting near a trash can, and if nothing else, it makes your bag less heavy to carry.

IT'S EASIER TO KEEP UP THAN CATCH UP.

By establishing helpful habits, we can cope with clutter little by little, as it comes into our surroundings, instead of trying to deal with it in big, heroic catch-up bursts.

BEWARE THE OFFICE BACKWATER.

Five pairs of shoes, four sweaters, seven plastic food containers, three gym bags . . . we bring things into work but neglect to take them home again, so they stagnate, forgotten. This pattern creates clutter at the office and inconvenience at home.

Each evening, check your workspace for anything that you need to take with you.

Consider keeping a "belongs elsewhere" box or shelf where such items can be stored until you're ready to retrieve them on your way out the door.

FEELING WAKEFUL?
TRY CLEARING CLUTTER.

Sleep experts suggest that when people have trouble sleeping, rather than toss and turn and fret, it's helpful to get out of bed for some quiet activity.

When I can't sleep, I find it helpful to clear some clutter. Nothing too taxing, nothing that takes much thought — but I'll wander around the apartment and put away anything that's out of place. I usually find plenty to keep me busy for twenty minutes and then I'm ready to head back to bed. It's a calming middle-of-the-night activity, and if I wake up exhausted the next day, at least my apartment looks good.

TO SAVE SPACE, STORE SHOES IN THE YIN-YANG POSITION.

SHOP SMART.

For some people, the habit of shopping leads to clutter problems. If so, try adopting these shopping habits:

- Don't walk into a store unless you're looking for a specific item.
- Be quick. The longer you stay in a store, the more you spend.
- Don't take a cart or a basket. You buy less if you have to carry things around in your arms.
- Touching or tasting things triggers the impulse to buy, so pass up the free samples.
- Watch out when you're near the register, an area packed with tempting impulse purchases.
- Erase your online accounts so you have to make the effort to reenter all your information with every purchase.
- Remember: Nothing's a bargain if you don't really need or want it.

I love a broad margin to my life.

HENRY DAVID THOREAU

FIX YOUR DESK TO
FOCUS YOUR MIND.

When we're juggling tasks at work, it's easy to get swamped by materials related to multiple unrelated projects.

It's tempting to say, "While I'm doing a bit of online research for this project, I might as well look up information for that other project." But this kind of disjointed work can make us feel overwhelmed and unproductive.

Instead, decide the priority for the next slot of time, and get out materials related only to that project. Put everything else out of sight and out of mind.

While you're at it, clear your computer, too, by closing anything on your screen that isn't directly relevant to your current project. Put your smartphone out of reach.

Use your desk to help you focus on a single active project.

CREATE A WAITING ROOM
FOR STUFF.

We all have items that are waiting to go someplace else: packages to be mailed, books to be returned to the library, a tennis racquet to be restrung.

Often, we just leave such things out on some table or counter with the thought, Well, I'll leave these shoes right here on the kitchen counter so that I remember to take them to get fixed. This can go on for *months.*

To address this mess, create a "waiting room" — a shelf in a closet, a corner of the garage — where such things can be properly stored as you prepare to deal with them.

Some people may want to be able to see the items in the waiting room, as a visual cue; others may prefer to have this waiting room hidden behind a door or in a drawer. Either approach works as long as you check that waiting room regularly and remember to deal with the items there.

CLEAN UP AFTER YOUR PET.
Make it a habit to put the dog toys away,
change the kitty litter, refresh the fish's
water, and deal with anything that looks
chewed up, scratched up, or outgrown.

PROCEED SOLO.

Sometimes, we feel like we can't start clearing clutter until everyone sharing our space agrees to participate.

Don't wait for other people's enthusiasm or cooperation. Do what's within your power solo.

You'll get the benefit of clearing your own clutter right away, without feeling frustrated by other people's attitudes.

Also, people often get inspired to clean up their own areas when they see other areas getting cleared. Example is more persuasive than admonition.

WHAT WE DO
EVERY DAY
MATTERS MORE THAN
WHAT WE DO
ONCE IN A WHILE.

DON'T LET YOURSELF
FALL INTO "EMPTY."

Keep cash in the house. Keep gas in your tank. Keep some extra rolls of toilet paper squirreled away. Keep your phone charged. Keep a sheet of stamps in a drawer.

You'll save time and avoid frustration.

CAST YOUR NET FOR CLUTTER MORE THAN ONCE.

Whenever you're finished with a particular instance of clutter-clearing, go back through the area you've covered — at least once or twice more.

There's something about clearing clutter that loosens our grip on our possessions. The first time you sort through that closet or that file folder, you'll get rid of a certain number of things. Then, when you go back for a second or third wave of clutter-clearing, you'll get rid of more.

As we let go of things, it feels more and more possible — and more and more enticing — to let go of more.

HAVE ENOUGH HANGERS, AND NO MORE THAN FIVE EXTRA HANGERS, IN EVERY CLOSET.

SORT THE MAIL REGULARLY.

Don't let the mail stack up in some corner. Mail is messy, and important letters can get lost.

If possible, get rid of junk mail as soon as it arrives. Move the useful mail (a far smaller stack) to some kind of holding area. I have a special drawer where I keep any mail that needs to be processed — bills to be paid, invitations to be answered, school info to add to my file — along with envelopes, stamps, checkbooks, and a return-address stamp. Then, every Sunday night, I watch TV and deal with the mail pile from my special drawer.

Everything gets dealt with regularly; the mail is safe yet out of sight until I'm ready to tackle it; it's easy to find anything I'm looking for.

Observe a "Power Hour."

Most of us have a long list of unpleasant chores that aren't urgent, so we just keep postponing them. Over time, this procrastination drains us.

To tackle this problem, try scheduling a "power hour." Make a list of all the tasks you'd like to accomplish, and once a week, for just one hour, steadily work on these chores.

Little by little, we can get a lot accomplished.

Use Hooks Instead of Hangers.

In many situations, it's much quicker and easier to put something on a hook, and when it's quicker and easier to keep a habit, we're far more likely to stick with it. So add hooks if possible.

MAKE YOUR BED.

When I ask people what habits make them happier, I'm surprised by how many answer, "Making my bed." Why does such an ordinary activity strike such a chord?

Making the bed is a quick and manageable task, yet it makes a room look much nicer.

Also, the bedroom plays a special part in our home; our bed is a symbol of *ourselves*. So when the bedroom seems better ordered, we feel better ordered.

Some people say that, to the contrary, they revel in *not* making their beds. Fair enough! Everyone's happiness project is different.

IF YOU CAN'T FIND SOMETHING, CLEAN UP.

This is astonishingly effective.

DON'T STOCKPILE.

It's easy to get into the habit of saving every rubber band, promotional mug, or baseball cap that you acquire — but don't stockpile more than you can reasonably use. Decide how many backups you need and don't accumulate too many extras.

Keep only a few shoeboxes, shoe bags, and shopping bags (and don't store them in the valuable real estate of your clothes closet).

Watch out for accidental stockpiles. Have you somehow amassed four jars of coriander or nine cheap conference tote bags?

The mere fact that you've acquired a sizable collection can make something seem more valuable. "I can't put ten years' worth of *National Geographic*s in the recycling bin!" But if you don't look at those magazines, they're clutter.

If possible, take steps to avoid acquiring these items at all. For instance, if you find you're amassing big quantities of ketchup packets or plastic utensils, ask for "food only" when you order takeout.

Have a purpose for your possessions. Don't get into the habit of keeping things for which you have no use.

GO SHELF BY SHELF.

Whenever you have a few minutes of idle time, take a moment to evaluate some small area. Okay, it's time to throw out the grapes that have gone wrinkly. Admit it, there's no reason to keep that hairbrush with the broken handle. That camera cord belongs in the camera-cord basket.

The shelf-by-shelf resolution has two advantages: it doesn't take much time and the results start to show very fast. You can fight a surprising amount of clutter without setting aside a big block of time to deal with it.

GET RID OF SOMETHING AS SOON AS IT BECOMES WORTHLESS.

I was on a sailboat when a friend's shoe fell overboard. He immediately picked up the matching shoe and tossed it into the water. I remember feeling shocked, by both the deliberate littering and the decision to throw away that second shoe. He was wrong to litter, but he was right that the unmatched shoe no longer had any value.

Remind yourself: Even if it's otherwise perfectly "good," you can't use a blender without a handle or a paper shredder that doesn't turn on. The broken umbrella, that dry Magic Marker, the outgrown dog collar from your dog's puppy days, the hair dryer that makes an ominous buzzing sound — you're not going to use these things. Get rid of them.

End Each Stage of Your Day with the "Ten-Minute Closer."

We give children transition times to help them move from one activity to the next, and adults benefit from transitions as well.

Before you leave work, take ten minutes to put things in order. This transition time helps to mark the end of the day — and it also makes it far more pleasant to return in the morning.

- Glance over your calendar for the next day (this step has saved me a lot of trouble)
- Throw away trash, such as food wrappers or dry pens, and remove dirty dishes
- Put loose change in a change cup
- Stash pens, paper clips, binder clips, rubber bands, and other supplies (by the end of the day, I have seven pens scattered across my desk)
- File or discard any papers that you no longer need
- Close any open drawers or doors
- Shred

Put away anything set in a transitional space, such as folders "temporarily" placed on the floor

Pack up anything that belongs at home

For extra credit:

Do a ten-minute email blast. For ten minutes, go as fast as you can through your email inbox and blast out as many responses as you can. Unsubscribe to any unwanted email newsletters.

Set up for the next day by gathering any necessary items (an especially good idea if you are sometimes late for work)

Before walking away from your workspace, take a moment to revel at how orderly and clear it looks.

At the end of the evening, do a ten-minute closer at home.

Put shoes away

Hang up coats

Close all drawers, closets, cabinets, and doors

Shove chairs back into place

Wipe the kitchen counters

Put dishes in the dishwasher

- Put newspapers and magazine in the recycling pile (if, like me, you're old-fashioned enough to read paper newspapers)
- Set the TV remote control back in its holder
- Toss junk mail
- Unpack any delivered packages
- Before walking to your bedroom, take a moment to revel at how orderly and clear your home looks.

PUT THINGS AWAY NEAR WHERE THEY WANT TO BE.

It's an odd phenomenon: some objects seem to want to live in a certain place. They naturally gravitate there, no matter what. If you find yourself moving an item from point A to point C, over and over, figure out whether you can store this item at point A or at least at point B.

It's easy to decide that an object "belongs" somewhere, but nothing *must* be kept in a certain place. You may think your robe belongs on a hook in the bathroom, but if your robe seems determined to make its home in the TV room, maybe you should let it live there instead.

REMIND YOURSELF, "I HAVE PLENTY OF ROOM FOR THE THINGS THAT ARE IMPORTANT TO ME."

The point of cultivating habits for continuous clutter-clearing isn't to achieve some particular level of perfection. It's to create an environment where we can feel, "I have plenty of room for the things that are important to me. I can find those things, I can see them, and if something new comes into my life, I have room to expand."

■ ■ ■ ■

5
ADD BEAUTY

■ ■ ■ ■

To know what to leave out
and what to put in;
just where and just how,
ah, *that* is to have been
educated in knowledge
of simplicity.
FRANK LLOYD WRIGHT

Having made choices,
created order, learned about
ourselves, and mastered
helpful habits, we've gone
far to beat clutter.

But to create outer order and inner calm, it's not enough to eliminate clutter; we want our surroundings to be *beautiful.*

We have paradoxical desires for our surroundings. We want a sense of abundance and plenty, and also of order and spaciousness. We want to feel both calmer and more energized. We want a quiet retreat for privacy and also a convivial center for hospitality.

With color, scent, space, light, and display, we can work a transformation. We can ensure that our places feel well used and valued, with no neglected corners, unusable areas, overflowing shelves, or nasty places. That new order creates a sensation of renewal.

We can curate our possessions to spotlight the people, places, and activities that we love.

And once that beauty is created, it's important to revel in it — to experience the inner calm that flows from outer order. Now that I don't spend time hunting for my missing gloves every morning, I can use that time to savor my first cup of coffee.

Add beauty.

CHOOSE A SIGNATURE COLOR.

It can be fun, and add to the beauty and harmony of your home, if you cultivate a certain shade of chartreuse, aquamarine, olive, or slate and make it "your" color.

A signature color makes decision-making easier. What color should you choose for your cell phone case or your exercise clothes? Your signature color, of course.

And seeing splashes of a color you love will raise your spirits.

Or maybe you don't have a signature color — maybe you have a signature pattern, like polka dots, stripes, animal print, or paisley, or a signature material, like denim, leather, or velvet.

To Get It Done, Make It *Fun.*

As Mary Poppins famously says, "In every job that must be done, there is an element of fun. You find the fun and — snap! The job's a game."

Use your imagination to turn your clutter-clearing session into a game. Beat your best time for cleaning the kitchen. Pretend to be someone hired from an outside cleaning service. Challenge yourself to toss ten items during a commercial break. Listen to your favorite upbeat music while you sort through piles. Listen to your favorite podcast while you fold laundry. Embrace the pleasurable destruction of shredding, throwing junk mail into the recycling bin, or feeding the garbage disposal.

Or turn clutter-clearing into a fun event. A friend works in a profession where she receives mounds of gifts every holiday season, and after every family Christmas dinner, she fills a side table with the items she doesn't want and announces, "Help yourself!" Her guests are thrilled by the things they find, and she puts nice possessions into the hands of people who will appreciate them.

SOMETIMES
MATERIAL DESIRES
HAVE A
SPIRITUAL ASPECT.

Consider a Child-Free Zone.

If you live with children and if your home is big enough, you may want to create a child-free zone.

Children like to run around, make noise, and make a mess. Their belongings seem to spread everywhere.

For this reason, try to create at least one child-free zone — a space where children aren't allowed to go without permission. Maybe it's your bedroom, maybe it's the living room, maybe it's a corner of a room.

Ideally, it's a place where adults can find privacy, order, and quiet when they need a respite from children's activities.

ENLARGE YOUR WORK SPACE.

Many of us spend time in workplaces that feel cramped. While it's easy to dream about more elbow room, we can make our current workplace feel more inviting and spacious by clearing clutter.

First, tackle your own space. Be ruthless about clearing your desk, computer desktop, shelves, drawers, and cabinets of anything you don't need, don't use, or don't love.

Then, consider whether you might be able to convince your coworkers to join in the effort.

By clearing out whatever has accumulated at the tops of bookshelves and cabinets, under desks, in corners, in hallways, on notice-boards, and on every flat surface, everyone in the whole office will gain more breathing room.

Your workplace might even designate a chief order officer, to give someone the specific responsibility and authority to tackle office disorder.

Space is beautiful.

SPEND OUT.

Do you have the impulse to save things, to hold back? I sure do.

I loved my delicate white wedding china so much that I used it only a handful of times during the first twenty years of married life, for fear that I'd break a plate or chip a bowl. Finally, I decided to face my fear, use the china, and enjoy it as long as it lasted.

Beautiful stationery, fancy bath salts, fine cooking ingredients, fresh new white T-shirts, sharp tools, piles of unread books . . . these things are meant to be put to work.

It's satisfying to use the things we own, and it's wasteful to save them for a day that may never come. Recently, I had to toss an expensive scented candle, still untouched inside its wrapper; I'd "saved" it for so long that the oils had separated and leaked. Why was I saving it?

Put things to good use. Spend out.

TIRED OF YOUR PLACE?
CREATE SOME OUTER ORDER.

During college, a friend lived off campus. At the end of our senior year, after she'd frantically cleaned her apartment to get her deposit back, she told me something I've always remembered.

"Don't wait to clean your apartment," she said. "I thought I didn't really like this place. But now that it's in such good shape, I realize how nice it was all along."

Often, when we want to make a change or improve an experience, we think, I need to do something drastic. Like move somewhere new.

Sometimes that's true. But sometimes we can take steps to improve our situation right now, within the bounds of our present experience. If we clean the apartment now, we might find that it's nicer than we thought.

USE MORE BY HAVING LESS.

One of the most pleasant aspects of clearing clutter is that once we get rid of things we don't use, need, or love, we boost our enjoyment of what we have.

After I've cleared out my closet, I find it much easier to get dressed and I wear a wider variety of outfits, because I like all the clothes I own and can find everything easily.

Every time I clear out my children's belongings, they suddenly have more fun with what they keep. They have more space to spread out, they can find the things they like more easily, and the process of clearing clutter reacquaints them with forgotten possessions.

Having less often leads us to use our things more often and with more enjoyment, because we're not fighting our way through a welter of unwanted stuff.

WATCH YOUR LANGUAGE.

The vocabulary that we choose influences how we perceive a task.

On your file folders, you might update the label CONTACTS to read FRIENDS AND FAMILY, or you might change the label of ARTICLES TO READ to TRAVEL AND VACATION.

On your calendar, you might write "Play piano" instead of "Practice piano," or "Email time" could become "Engagement time." You might schedule a "personal retreat day," a "catch-up day," a "ditch day," or a "mandatory vacation day."

Instead of telling yourself, "I need to go through my photos and discard the bad ones," you could tell yourself, "I'm going to curate my photo collection."

Different vocabulary appeals to different people; speak to yourself in language that you find most compelling.

CULTIVATE AN
ATTITUDE OF GRATITUDE.

Sometimes our stuff drives us a little crazy, so it's helpful to stay grateful to our possessions: for having served us well, for embodying someone else's affection for us in the form of a gift, or for giving us a thrill upon purchase.

And most important, we should be grateful that we're lucky enough to have these things in our lives.

An attitude of gratitude, even for inanimate objects, makes us happier.

EMBARRASSED?

Are you embarrassed by any item you possess? It's a bad feeling. Take steps to fix it, clean it, or get rid of it.

MAKE LIVING SPACES MORE LIVABLE.

If you don't use an area, why not?

Do you avoid your desk because it's too far away from the activity of the house — or too close to the activity of the house? Do you find yourself sitting in the kitchen instead of in the living room because the living room is too crowded — or too bare? Do you dislike reading in the armchair because the light isn't good or because there's no place to put your coffee mug?

Walk through a room that's underused and ask yourself, "What could I do to make this area more attractive?" Figure out what's needed to make the room more inviting: more light, plants, art, bookshelves, photographs, footstools, side tables? Do the items on the shelves need to be more carefully chosen? Does the furniture need to be more comfortable?

But be honest with yourself. If you prefer to work in bed, rather than at a desk, fixing up your desk doesn't matter much.

ADD A TOUCH OF LUXURY.

Just a little luxury can add beauty to our lives.

A set of gorgeous colored markers, an excellent chef's knife, Egyptian cotton sheets, a wallet made of the finest leather, a really good umbrella . . . a splurge in the right area can make our lives much more pleasant. When my husband developed a taste for bourbon, I bought him two crystal glasses to add to his enjoyment of the drink.

We can add a touch of luxury at work, too. Using exceptionally well-made tools or introducing a note of whimsy makes work more pleasant. For my own office, to put the "fun" in "functional," I chose file folders printed in bright patterns, sticky notes decorated with a playful design, and an elegant book weight.

These tools — which are nicer than they strictly need to be — help me enjoy my work.

CHOOSE THE BIGGER LIFE.

When trying to make a tough choice, challenge yourself: "Choose the bigger life."

The helpful thing about this question is that it reveals our values. Different people have different views on what the "bigger life" would include.

For instance, when my family was debating whether we should get a dog, I was suspended between the pros and the cons — until I thought, Choose the bigger life. For us, choosing the bigger life meant getting a dog. And we're so, so happy with our dog, Barnaby.

For someone else, choosing the bigger life might mean *not* getting a dog, and by not getting a dog, that person would be able to travel for long periods or have more money to spend.

By choosing the bigger life, we make space for our lives to expand in a new direction.

MAKE AN ENTRANCE.

When people walk through the door, they want to dump their bags, kick off their shoes, and drop their coats. This means that entrances tend to become cluttered and chaotic.

Which is an overwhelming sight, and very uninviting.

Make it easy to put things away. Think about how hooks, baskets, bowls, or shelves could help maintain order. Add some art, a plant, a mural, or an attractive piece of furniture to make the space more beautiful. Stay vigilant so things don't stay out of place overnight.

We want to feel a sense of sanctuary and calm when we step over our own threshold.

CREATE A SEASONAL PHOTO GALLERY.

Few things make us happier than looking at photographs of the people we love. At the same time, it's all too easy for a mantelpiece, side table, or bulletin board to get crowded with photos that are so familiar that we don't even see them anymore.

To fight this familiarity, create a set of photos that are displayed only at certain times. A Christmas photo display, or a Fourth of July display, or a back-to-school display.

You might want to get themed frames. For my family's Valentine's Day gallery, I've chosen pink, red, and silver frames, and the gallery makes a festive holiday decoration.

Because these photos are on view for a short time, they don't fade into the background as other photos tend to do. And having these seasonal displays makes it easier to winnow down the photos crammed into other areas.

Everything Looks Better Arranged on a Tray.

Perfume bottles. Spice jars. Cuff links. Enamel boxes. Coffee-making materials.

A tray (or a basket, bowl, or plate) pulls individual items into a pleasing collection.

Even when things are in the right place, they may look messy and scattered until they're contained in some way.

BRING QUIET TO VISUAL NOISE.
Certain areas can get so crowded and "loud" that they hurt the eye.

At home, a refrigerator door that's plastered with school schedules, children's artwork, expired coupons, magazine clippings, tattered flyers, and rubbery magnets is neither a helpful resource nor a place of beauty, and it will make the kitchen seem messy, even if everything else is beautifully ordered.

At work, a computer screen framed with dozens of scrawled sticky-note reminders creates visual cacophony.

Try to bring down the noise level.

LIGHT SOME CANDLES.

Candles are easy and inexpensive, and add great elegance to a room — and the slight flickering motion adds a sense of life.

Scented candles can add a beautiful fragrance as well.

INCLUDE A FRAGMENT OF NATURE.
Shells, pebbles, flowers, driftwood, sea glass, pinecones, hollow birds' eggs, a fern frond pressed against glass . . . there's something very satisfying about seeing the outdoors come indoors. Nature has its own deep order.

ASK YOURSELF, "DOES THIS POSSESSION *SPARK JOY* IN ME?" OR "DOES THIS POSSESSION *ENERGIZE* ME?"

Marie Kondo's blockbuster bestseller *The Life-Changing Magic of Tidying Up* persuaded many people to clear clutter.

Readers seemed most inspired by her suggestion to keep only those possessions that "spark joy." Kondo explains, "The best way to choose what to keep and what to throw away is to take each item in one's hand and ask: 'Does this spark joy?' If it does, keep it. If not, dispose of it."

Or for people (like me) who don't find that question particularly helpful, try, "Does this energize me?" For me, focusing on "energy" rather than "joy" provides more clarity.

Enjoy What's Special about Your Space.

When choosing where to live, you were probably drawn to certain features of your home — the deck, the fireplace, the garden, the porch, the sunroom.

Now that you actually live in that place, do you use that feature? If not, can you take some steps to make it easier to enjoy it?

You can't enjoy the sitting room if you've tossed the junk from the rest of the house in there. You can't enjoy the deck if the outdoor furniture never leaves the garage. You paid dearly for your apartment's private balcony, but it has become the dumping area for your old bike and half-dead plants.

Enjoy what you have.

Probably one can say
that all beautiful,
noble, or brilliant works are of use,
or that everything that
proves to be useful
or beneficial
has its own beauty.

ISAK DINESEN

Every Room Should Include Something Purple.

Or something glittery, or something miniature or oversize, or in a striking pattern, or something ugly.

That is, every room should hold a bit of surprise or whimsy.

Someplace, Keep an Empty Shelf; Someplace, Keep a Junk Drawer.

My empty shelf gives me the luxury of space; I have room for more things to come into my life. It feels almost decadent to reserve space for beautiful emptiness.

My junk drawer makes room for the things that don't have an obvious place in my home, but for some reason I want to keep. I want an orderly home, but I want to make room for a little bit of messy.

I love my empty shelf, and I love my junk drawer.

CREATE OUTER ORDER ON YOUR SMARTPHONE.

Clear away the visual clutter on your smartphone.

Keep only the most essential apps on your first screen and move the others to later screens. Regularly delete apps you don't use.

To create even more space, use folders. For instance, by putting my travel-related apps in a TRAVEL folder, I opened up a lot of empty space.

For even more visual order, arrange your apps by color to make your display more pleasing to the eye, or arrange your apps by function to make it more efficient.

Adjust the notifications and sounds on your smartphone as well. When I turned off all sounds, and when I cut back on my notifications, my phone became a much less intrusive tool.

If someone asked me what my idea of luxury is, I think my answer would be: flowers in the house all year round.

MAY SARTON

CREATE A SECRET PLACE.

Make your home feel more alive by creating a secret place, known only to members of your household — whether it's a desk with a hidden drawer, or a concealed closet, or a locked chest.

In his brilliant book *A Pattern Language,* Christopher Alexander asks, "Where can the need for concealment be expressed; the need to hide; the need for something precious to be lost, and then revealed?"

As you clear clutter, you'll probably discover a place that could become a secret place. It's strangely satisfying.

SOMETIMES,
WE CAN MINISTER
TO THE SOUL
THROUGH THE BODY.

REMEMBER LOVE.

This is the most important suggestion of all.

When your parents are driving you crazy because they've kept every piece of your schoolwork back to kindergarten, or when you're driving yourself crazy because you can't bring yourself to toss your husband's ragged college T-shirts, remember: *All this junk is an expression of love.*

■ ■ ■ ■

CONCLUSION: THE FULFILLMENT OF INNER CALM

■ ■ ■ ■

Outer order is a challenge to impose and it's a chore to maintain. Nevertheless, for most of us, it's worth the effort.

Why? Why does outer order contribute to inner calm, and why does inner calm make us happier?

To answer these questions, it's helpful to think about the elements of a happy life: *feeling good, feeling bad,* and *feeling right,* in an *atmosphere of growth.*

- Outer order helps us to *feel good:* we gain a sense of rest, of spaciousness, of organization, of energy.
- Outer order helps us no longer to *feel bad:* we get relief from irritation, guilt, frustration, hurry, and resentment of other people.

- Outer order helps us to *feel right:* we're able to keep our attention, time, energy, and money trained on the tasks, people, places, activities, and values that matter most to us.
- Outer order helps us to create an *atmosphere of growth:* we make visible improvements in our surroundings, in ways that benefit everyone who enters that place, with room to expand, with a sense of renewal.

The irony is that just as outer order contributes to inner calm, inner calm contributes to outer order. When we feel serene, energetic, and focused, *that's* when it becomes easier to keep our surroundings in good order. It's a virtuous cycle.

For me — and for many other people — when it's easier for me to hang up my coat, it becomes easier to go to the gym. A clear desk helps me to write an unpleasant email with less waffling. Change fosters change.

Getting control of our possessions makes us feel more in control of our fates. If this is an illusion, it's a helpful illusion — and it's a more pleasant way to live.

And I think there's a second, more mysterious reason that outer order contributes to inner calm.

The association between outer order and inner calm runs deep. My possessions aren't me, that's true — yet it's also true that my possessions *are* me.

We extend ourselves into the things around us; we fashion our surroundings as snails build their shells. With our possessions, we make a mark upon the world. And whether this mark is grand or modest, whether this mark is made with possessions many or few, we want to create an environment that truly suits us.

When we look at our stuff, we see a reflection of ourselves. We're happier when that stuff is in good order and includes things that we need, use, and love — because that reflection influences the way we see *ourselves.*

Once outer order emerges, take the opportunity to enjoy it, to experience the ease, space, and growth that come from inner calm. Revel in it! Take time to pause and to feel happy.

ACKNOWLEDGMENTS

Thanks, as always, to my brilliant agent, Christy Fletcher.

Thanks to Crystal Ellefsen, whose remarkable insights and hard work allow me to put my words out into the world every day.

Thanks to Jayme Johnson and Jody Matchett for their indispensable help.

Thanks to my wonderful publishing team: Christina Foxley, Diana Baroni, Sarah Breivogel, Aaron Wehner, Danielle Deschenes, and Marysarah Quinn, and special thanks to my terrific editor, Mary Reynics.

Thanks to my readers, listeners, and viewers. I've gained so much from your insights, observations, and questions about outer order and inner calm.

A heartfelt thanks to my beloved family and friends, who are the beneficiaries — and the innocent bystanders — of my quest for outer order.

And finally, special thanks to my sister,

Elizabeth, who has given me so many hours of happiness by graciously allowing me to clear her clutter.

TOP TEN TIPS FOR CREATING OUTER ORDER

Everyone has a different list, of course. From my observations, these ten tips are the ones people find most useful:

1 | Make your bed.
2 | Follow the "one-minute rule" — anything you can do in less than one minute, do without delay.
3 | Have a weekly "power hour" — make a list of tasks you'd like to accomplish and spend one hour, once a week, tackling the items on the list.
4 | Make it fun to get the job done.
5 | Don't let yourself fall into "empty."
6 | Don't put things down, put them away.
7 | Don't stockpile; that is, don't store more of an item than you can realistically use.

8 | Keep mementos that are small in size and few in number.

9 | Keep things organized, but not overly organized.

10 | If you can't find something, clean up.

SUGGESTIONS FOR FURTHER READING

If you'd like to read more about creating outer order, you might enjoy these books.

THE HAPPINESS PROJECT by Gretchen Rubin

One rainy afternoon, while riding a city bus, I asked myself, "What do I want from life, anyway?" I thought, I want to be happy — yet I realized that I didn't spend any time thinking about my happiness. In a flash, I decided to dedicate a year to a "happiness project." I spent twelve months test-driving the wisdom of the ages, current scientific research, and lessons from popular culture about how to be happier. Each month, using myself as a guinea pig, I tested a new set of resolutions around different themes, such as vitality, leisure, and marriage.

HAPPIER AT HOME by Gretchen Rubin

This book is all about — you guessed it — how to be happier at home.

Starting in September (the other January), I dedicated a school year — September through May — to making my home a place of greater simplicity, comfort, and love. Each month, I tackled a different theme, such as possessions, time, and neighborhood, by experimenting with concrete, manageable resolutions aimed at making my home a happier place.

BETTER THAN BEFORE by Gretchen Rubin

When we're trying to create and maintain outer order, we often try to improve our habits. But *how* exactly do we change our habits?

Many experts offer one-size-fits-all solutions — but, alas, there's no magic formula that works for everyone. The secret is to pinpoint the specific strategies that will work for each of us. From finding the right time to begin a new habit, to recognizing the counterintuitive risks of reward, to using the pleasure of treats to strengthen our good habits, I identify the twenty-one strategies that will allow every reader to find an effective, individual fit.

A PATTERN LANGUAGE by Christopher Alexander et al.

This strange, brilliant book changed the way I see the world. It uses architecture, sociology, psychology, and anthropology to describe the most satisfying designs of towns, buildings, offices, and homes, by setting forth an archetypal "language" of 253 "patterns."

Instead of discussing familiar architectural styles and design decisions, it focuses on patterns such as the Front Door Bench, Child Caves, Sleeping to the East, Staircase as Stage, Cascade of Roofs, and Half-Hidden Garden. My favorite? Secret Place. As I explain in *Happier at Home,* I was inspired to create several secret places in our apartment. I couldn't stop with just one.

THE LIFE-CHANGING MAGIC OF TIDYING UP by Marie Kondo

This book made me jump out of my chair and start clearing clutter.

I don't believe that there's one "right" way to clear clutter; as I explore here, and in my other books, I believe that we all must find the way to happiness and good habits that's right for us. Kondo argues for one "best" way, the KonMari way. Nevertheless, I did find the book both engaging and helpful.

ORGANIZING FROM THE INSIDE OUT by Julia Morgenstern

This book is helpful, realistic, and concrete.

Julie Morgenstern emphasizes the *reasons* for clutter. The fact is, clutter isn't just a matter of not having enough closet space or not sorting the mail every day. She addresses the fact that we hold on to possessions for different reasons, and once we acknowledge that aspect of clutter, we're able to clear clutter far more effectively, by setting up systems that are suited to our own nature.

ABOUT THE AUTHOR

Gretchen Rubin is one of the most thought-provoking and influential writers on the linked subjects of happiness, habits, and human nature. She's the author of many books, including the blockbuster best-sellers *The Happiness Project, Better Than Before, The Four Tendencies,* and *Happier at Home.* She has an enormous following, in print and online, and her books have sold more than three million copies worldwide, in thirty languages. On her popular podcast *Happier with Gretchen Rubin,* she discusses happiness and good habits with her sister, Elizabeth Craft (Elizabeth is very messy), and on her site, gretchenrubin.com, she regularly reports on her adventures in pursuit of happiness. A graduate of Yale and Yale Law School, Gretchen Rubin was clerking for Supreme Court Justice Sandra Day O'Connor when she realized she wanted to be a writer. She lives in New York City with her husband and two daughters.

The employees of Thorndike Press hope you have enjoyed this Large Print book. All our Thorndike, Wheeler, and Kennebec Large Print titles are designed for easy reading, and all our books are made to last. Other Thorndike Press Large Print books are available at your library, through selected bookstores, or directly from us.

For information about titles, please call:
(800) 223-1244

or visit our website at:
gale.com/thorndike

To share your comments, please write:
Publisher
Thorndike Press
10 Water St., Suite 310
Waterville, ME 04901